Program of

Priestly

Formation

Fifth Edition

UNITED STATES CONFERENCE OF CATHOLIC BISHOPS

Washington, D.C.

The document *Program of Priestly Formation* (fifth edition) was developed by the Committee on Priestly Formation of the United States Conference of Catholic Bishops (USCCB). It was approved by the full body of bishops at its June 2005 General Meeting, received the subsequent *approbatio* of the Holy See, and has been authorized for publication by the undersigned.

Msgr. David J. Malloy, STD
General Secretary, USCCB

In 2001 the National Conference of Catholic Bishops (NCCB) and United States Catholic Conference (USCC) became the United States Conference of Catholic Bishops (USCCB).

First Printing, September 2006

ISBN 1-57455-517-0
ISBN 978-1-57455-517-2

Program of Priestly Formation

Contents

Decree of Promulgation.. vii

Statement from the Conference of
Major Superiors of Men.. viii

Foreword ix

Preface 1

Introduction.. 4

The Nature and Mission of the Ministerial Priesthood...................... 8

The Life of Priests 11

Priestly Vocations in the Church's Pastoral Work and
the Admission of Candidates.. 15

    Norms for the Admission of Candidates.................................... 21

The Formation of Candidates for Priesthood 28

    I. Human Formation 29

        Norms for Human Formation.. 36

    II. Spiritual Formation 42

        Norms for Spiritual Formation.. 48

    III. Intellectual formation 53

        Norms for Intellectual Formation 65

    IV. Pastoral Formation... 76

        Norms for Pastoral Formation... 82

    V. Community 85

        Norms for Community.. 87

    VI. The Continuing Evaluation of Seminarians............................ 89

        Norms for the Continuing Evaluation of Seminarians 89

Seminaries: Governance, Administration, and
Faculty Governance 97

Administration.. 102

The Ongoing Formation of Priests 113

Conclusion 116

Addendum A.
Norms Concerning Applications for
Priestly Formation from Those Previously Enrolled in
a Formation Program 117

Index 125

Decree of Promulgation

On June 16, 2005, the members of the United States Conference of Catholic Bishops approved the *Program of Priestly Formation* (fifth edition) as the *Ratio institutionis sacerdotalis* for the United States to be observed in seminaries for the formation of priests.

This action of the United States Conference of Catholic Bishops, made in accord with canon 242 §1 of the *Code of Canon Law*, was approved *ad quinquennium* by the Congregation for Catholic Education by a decree of November 15, 2005 (Prot. N. 1370/2003), signed by His Eminence, Zenon Cardinal Grocholewski, Prefect of the Congregation, and the Most Reverend J. Michael Miller, CSB, Secretary of the same Congregation.

As President of the United States Conference of Catholic Bishops, I therefore decree the promulgation of the *Program of Priestly Formation* (fifth edition), which is to be observed in all seminaries, whether diocesan or interdiocesan, from the date of this same decree.

Given at the offices of the United States Conference of Catholic Bishops in Washington, the District of Columbia, on the 4th day of August, in the year of our Lord 2006, the Feast of St. John Vianney.

✠ William S. Skylstad
Bishop of Spokane
President
United States Conference of Catholic Bishops

Monsignor David J. Malloy
General Secretary

Statement from the Conference of Major Superiors of Men

The Conference of Major Superiors of Men, recognizing its obligations to help ensure quality training and education for the ordained ministry, has over the past few years collaborated with the Bishops' Committee on Priestly Formation in revising the *Program of Priestly Formation*. We are pleased that the committee which drafted this revision of the document has included sections dealing with ordained ministry within the context of religious life. Although academic requirements may be similar for both religious and diocesan priests, the religious priest will understand the ordained role and ministry as reflecting the charism and spiritual traditions of his religious institute.

The Conference of Major Superiors of Men adopts the *Program of Priestly Formation* Fifth Edition as applicable to all religious seminaries in the United States. We do this at the invitation of the United States Conference of Catholic Bishops, preserving the rights and privileges granted religious in church law, especially regarding the religious and spiritual formation of their own candidates.

Foreword

Bishop George H. Niederauer, Chair of the Bishops' Committee on Priestly Formation (1999-2002), asked Bishop John C. Nienstedt in December 2001 to chair a subcommittee overseeing the first phase of the revision of the *Program of Priestly Formation*. Bishop Niederauer also asked bishops, major superiors, and seminary rectors to consult with others in their administration and to offer suggestions about a new edition of the *Program of Priestly Formation*. The long process of gathering these comments and suggestions produced a wealth of insights based on both experience and expertise, which helped to fashion the current fifth edition of the *Program of Priestly Formation*. This edition was also greatly influenced by the Apostolic Exhortation of John Paul II, *Pastores dabo vobis* (1992). It is with great joy that we present this document, which is the result of much consultation and collaboration and has involved the work of three bishops' committees on priestly formation. It is truly a witness to the importance of priestly formation in the Church.

The drafting committee for the *Program of Priestly Formation* included Bishop John C. Nienstedt, Chair; Archbishop Timothy Dolan; Bishop Gregory Aymond; Bishop Earl Boyea; Bishop Curtis Guillory, SVD; Bishop Kevin Rhoades; Fr. William J. Baer; Fr. Louis J. Cameli; Fr. Robert E. Manning, SJ; Fr. Daniel McLellan, OFM; Fr. Mark O'Keefe, OSB; and Abbot Nathan Zodrow, OSB. They were ably assisted by Msgr. Edward J. Burns, Mr. Jason Straczewski, and Mr. Jamie Blosser.

The members of the Bishops' Committee on Priestly Formation who brought the project to completion are Bishop Thomas J. Olmsted, Chair; Archbishop Basil Schott, OFM; Archbishop Edwin F. O'Brien; Bishop Earl Boyea; Bishop Edward K. Braxton; and Bishop Felipe de Jesus Estevez. In his November 15, 2005, letter to Bishop Skylstad (Prot. 1370/2003), President of the USCCB, His Eminence Zenon Cardinal Grocholewski stated that "the Congregation for Catholic education has completed its study of the Fifth Edition of the *Program of Priestly Formation*, which is destined for use in the seminaries of the United States. The text is most appropriate. Of special benefit, in fact, will be the increased requirements for philosophical studies to a minimum of thirty credits and the lengthening of the pre-theology period to a minimum of two calendar years. . . .

We are now happy to approve the Fifth Edition of the *Program of Priestly Formation* for a period of five years." With the successful completion of this document, the Bishops' Committee on Priestly Formation is pleased to offer this *Program of Priestly Formation* with much gratitude for all those who participated in the consultation.

On behalf of the United States Conference of Catholic Bishops and the Bishops' Committee on Priestly Formation, I offer our prayers and support for all those who play an important part in the vital work of priestly formation.

✠ Thomas J. Olmsted
Chairman, Bishops' Committee on Priestly Formation

Preface

1.   The fifth edition of the *Program of Priestly Formation* of the United States Conference of Catholic Bishops (USCCB) builds upon the foundation of previous editions. The principal and new direction of the fifth edition stems from its reliance on the Post-Synodal Apostolic Exhortation *Pastores dabo vobis* (*I Will Give You Shepherds: On the Formation of Priests in the Circumstances of the Present Day*, 1992) to organize and integrate the program of priestly formation. Two other papal documents also enter into the vision and shaping of priestly formation: *Novo millennio ineunte* (*At the Close of the Great Jubilee of the Year 2000*, 2001) and *Ecclesia in America* (*The Church in America*, 1999).

2.   Documents of the Second Vatican Council establish a normative understanding of the presbyteral office.[1] They form an essential resource for the program of priestly formation along with the Council's specific treatment of priestly formation found in *Optatam totius* (*Decree on the Training of Priests*). After the Council, the Church laid down norms to aid national conferences in developing programs of priestly formation for given nations or rites. These norms were contained in the *Ratio fundamentalis institutionis sacerdotalis* (1970), which was revised and reissued in 1985 in light of the revision of the *Code of Canon Law* (1983). The *Code of Canon Law* and the *Code of Canons of the Eastern Churches* (1990), the *Ratio fundamentalis* (1985), and the *Catechism of the Catholic Church* (CCC, 1993), as an authentic articulation of the Church's faith, shape the current *Program of Priestly Formation* (PPF).

---

1   Among these, of special importance are *Lumen gentium* (*Dogmatic Constitution on the Church*); *Christus Dominus* (*Decree on the Pastoral Office of the Bishop*); and *Presbyterorum ordinis* (*Decree on the Ministry and Life of Priests*).

3.　　Other documents of the Holy See pertaining to priestly formation and treating specific aspects of seminary programs contribute to the PPF.[2] The Bishops' Committee on Priestly Formation has published documents identifying particular concerns and giving specific directions in light of needs and experiences in the United States.[3] The Bishops' Committee on Priestly Life and Ministry has also contributed a series of important documents on priestly ministry and life that also influence the PPF.[4]

4.　　In addition to documents, the various editions of the PPF, including this one, have benefited immensely from direct reflection on seminary formation through a series of visitations. A pattern of episcopal oversight was developed after the Council through seminary visitations organized by the USCCB. In 1981, Pope John Paul II mandated an apostolic visitation of all United States seminaries. The visitations resulted in observations published by the Congregation for Catholic Education on freestanding diocesan seminary theologates (1986), college seminaries (1988), and religious priestly formation (1990) in collaboration with the Congregation for the Institutes of Consecrated Life and Societies of Apostolic Life. These observations played an important role in shaping the fourth edition of the PPF.

5.　　From 1995 until the present, there has been a series of voluntary seminary visitations. Results of these visitations have entered into the formulation of the current, fifth edition of the PPF.[5]

2　　The Holy See has given direction on the teaching of philosophy (1972), theology (1976), canon law (1975), mutual relations between bishops and religious (1978), liturgical formation (1979), social communications (1986), pastoral care of people on the move (1986), Oriental Churches (1987), social doctrine (1988), Mariology (1988), patristics (1989), formation in religious institutes (1990), marriage (1995), ecumenism (1998), *Fraternal Life in Community* (1994), and the interrelation of theology and philosophy (1998). The Congregation for Catholic Education has also commented on other aspects of formation, notably celibacy (1974), *Sapientia christiana* (1979), and spiritual formation (1980).

3　　Documents, for example, on spiritual formation (1983), liturgy (1984), and pastoral formation (1985).

4　　Documents, for example, on preaching (1982), stress (1982), sexuality (1983), general health of priests (1983), ongoing formation (1984), the role of pastor (1987), morale (1989), and a basic plan for the ongoing formation of priests (2001).

5　　For a synthesis, see Fr. Edward J. Burns, Executive Director of the Bishops' Committee on Priestly Formation, "The Voluntary U.S. Seminary Visitations in Recent Years," *Origins* Vol. 32/ No. 20 (October 24, 2002), 332-335. Some of the findings highlighted by the visitations included these needs: for faculty to reflect the diversity of the student body; special care for the ongoing formation of faculty; clear criteria for admissions; a more precise determination of how the results of psychological testing are shared; for seminaries to develop handbooks; a retention of a full, uncompromised pre-theology program; finding ways to bring out the pastoral and priestly dimensions of classroom material; attention to the ecumenical and interfaith dimensions of theology; special attention to the formation of spiritual directors; an identification of elements of a spiritual formation; the integration of celibacy formation in the entire program; and linking theological reflection to the formation process.

6.   In the current edition of the PPF, the bishops of the United States have taken the directions and vision of the Holy See and reflected on the lived experience of seminaries in the United States and then formulated this edition of the program. The PPF, then, is normative for United States seminary programs and serves as a basis for future visitations.[6] At the same time, each seminary, with the approval of the diocesan bishop or the bishops concerned, or of the religious superior as the case may be, is to develop, articulate, and implement its own particular program in conformity with the PPF.

---

6   See *Codex Iuris Canonici* (CIC) (*Code of Canon Law*), Latin-English Edition (Washington, DC: Canon Law Society of America, 1998), c. 455 and c. 242. This *Program of Priestly Formation* is intended to serve the entire Catholic Church in the United States. Some of its principles, norms, and pastoral applications are specific to the Latin Rite. Nonetheless, the *Program for Priestly Formation* is also normative for all Eastern Churches *sui iuris* in the United States except where it conflicts with their particular traditions and pastoral life, and with the requirements of the *Codex Canonum Ecclesiarum Orientalium* (CCEO) (*Code of Canons of the Eastern Churches*) (Washington, DC: Canon Law Society of America, 2001).

Introduction

PRIESTLY FORMATION: IN COMMUNION WITH JESUS AND PARTICIPATION IN HIS MISSION

7.   Pope John Paul II describes seminary formation as "a continuation in the Church of the apostolic community gathered about Jesus, listening to his word, proceeding towards the Easter experience, awaiting the gift of the Spirit for the mission."[7]

8.   Priestly formation today continues the call of Jesus, the response of his first disciples, and their communion of life. The Gospel foundation of priestly formation precedes programs, structures, and plans. What was vital and essential for that first community of disciples remains so today for those engaged in priestly formation:

> As he was walking by the Sea of Galilee, he saw two brothers, Simon who is called Peter, and his brother Andrew, casting a net into the sea; they were fishermen. He said to them, "Come after me, and I will make you fishers of men." At once, they left their nets and followed him. (Mt 4:18-20)

9.   The Church continues to place the highest value on the work of priestly formation, because it is linked to the very mission of the Church, especially the evangelization of humanity:[8] "Go, therefore, and make disciples of all nations" (Mt 28:19). Our apostolic origins, which bind us in communion with the Lord and his mission, motivate those who engage in the ministry of priestly formation, underscore the urgency of their task, and remind them of their great responsibility. This same sense of urgency and responsibility helps shape the PPF.

---

7   John Paul II, *Pastores dabo vobis* (*I Will Give You Shepherds: On the Formation of Priests in the Circumstances of the Present Day*) (Washington, DC: United States Conference of Catholic Bishops, 1992), no. 60. Some subsequent references will be given in the text.

8   See *Pastores dabo vobis*, no. 2.

PRIESTLY FORMATION: IN A CONTEXT OF THE WORLD AND CHURCH TODAY

10.   Priestly formation takes place in a given ecclesial and historical context. Identifying that context is a critical task for giving specific shape to particular programs of formation. The importance of context is highlighted in *Pastores dabo vobis*: "God always calls his priests from specific human and ecclesial contexts, which inevitably influence them; and to these same contexts the priest is sent for the service of Christ's Gospel" (*Pastores dabo vobis*, no. 5).

11.   Although much could be said about the general context of priestly formation in the Church today, two points of particular importance emerge, and they are results or fruits of the worldwide celebration of the Great Jubilee.

- The Church reclaimed with greater clarity and vigor the mandate to continue the authentic renewal inaugurated by the Second Vatican Council, recognizing that the Council itself was "the great grace bestowed on the Church in the twentieth century."[9]
- With a renewed sense of mission, the Church wants to engage in the *new evangelization* by rekindling "in ourselves the impetus of the beginnings and allow[ing] ourselves to be filled with the ardor of the apostolic preaching which followed Pentecost."[10]

12.   There are also many significant elements of context particular to the United States at the beginning of the twenty-first century. These elements ought to play an important part in shaping seminary formation today, and they set the horizon for priestly ministry in the years ahead. Here we can name some of the more significant elements of context.

- In the United States at this time, there is the paradox of a widespread thirst for spirituality and, at the same time, a prevailing secular ethos. From another perspective, the nation finds itself more intensely called to build a "civilization of life and love," even as it struggles against a "culture of death."

---

9   John Paul II, *Novo millennio ineunte* (At the Close of the Great Jubilee of the Year 2000) (Vatican City: Libreria Editrice Vaticana, 2001), no. 57, http://www.vatican.va/holy_father/john_paul_ii/apost_letters/documents/hf_jp-ii_apl_20010106_novo-millennio-ineunte_en.html (accessed July 2006).

10   *Novo millennio ineunte*, no. 40.

- Weaknesses of ethical standards and a moral relativism have a corrosive effect on American public life as seen, for example, in marriage and family life, in business, and in politics. This ethical environment has affected the Church herself, for example, as seen in the scandalous behavior of some clergy who have abused minors and engaged in sexual misconduct, causing great suffering for the victims and damaging the Church's witness in society. Both the nation and the Church in the nation are summoned to renewal and to a greater integrity of life. The *Charter for the Protection of Young People* and the *Essential Norms* adopted by the Catholic bishops in the United States in 2002 (revised in 2005) provide an example of moving in this direction.
- In United States society at large, many persons are unchurched or unaffiliated with any denomination or faith tradition but remain open to evangelization.
- There are large numbers of inactive or "semi-active" Catholics as well as poorly catechized Catholics who need to be called back to full participation in the life of the Church.
- The Catholic Church in the United States continues to be firmly committed to and engaged in ecumenical and interreligious dialogue and cooperation.
- Globalization has underscored the need for greater coordination and deeper communion with the Church in other parts of the world. *Ecclesia in America* bears witness to this reality and responsibility, especially in our own hemisphere.
- In most dioceses in the United States, the norm is a high level of cultural, linguistic, and economic diversity. A new wave of Catholic immigration has located numerous newly arrived people who present their own economic and religious issues alongside numerous other Catholic laity who are native-born and are already economically and religiously established. Both groups share a common Church, have very different backgrounds, and can be mutually enriched by the exchange of their gifts.
- The greater diversity of candidates for priestly ministry also forms an important context for the Church and for priestly formation. They may be, for example:
  — Older men who bring previous life and work experiences
  — Candidates born outside the United States who speak English as a second language

— Candidates whose faith has been rediscovered and rekindled in a powerful way through significant religious experiences

— Candidates born and raised in the United States who find themselves struggling intensely with particular cultural counterpoints to the Gospel, especially regarding sexual permissiveness, the drive to acquire and consume material resources, and the exaltation of freedom as merely personal and individual autonomy, divorced from personal responsibility and objective moral standards

• An increasing number of priestly vocations now come from diverse and sometimes dysfunctional family situations.

• The demographics of the Catholic Church in the United States demonstrate the challenging situation of fewer priests and a growing Catholic population.

• The ministerial collaboration of priests with bishops, other priests, deacons, religious, and laity has become an important feature of church life in the United States.

• Continuing and, sometimes, significant differences about what is essential to Catholic belief have strained many dimensions of church life, diminishing the impact of the mission of the Church on society.

• At the same time, the hope and promise of a new springtime for the Catholic Church in the United States, a fruit of the Great Jubilee, has also offered a more positive context for vocations.

The Nature and Mission of the Ministerial Priesthood

INTRODUCTION

13.   All priestly formation must have its foundation in an adherence to the truths of faith about the nature and mission of the ministerial priesthood. Those who are involved in the process of priestly formation whether as administrators, teachers, formators, or seminarians must adhere to these teachings.

TRUTH

14.   All priestly formation must be firmly grounded in the truths of the Catholic faith, for it is from these truths that the nature and mission of the ministerial priesthood are drawn. Likewise, it is critical that formators and seminarians keep returning to the core of the faith for the integrating vision necessary for the full realization of the four dimensions of formation: human, spiritual, intellectual, and pastoral.

TRINITARIAN FOUNDATIONS

15.   *Pastores dabo vobis* delineates the Trinitarian foundations of the ministerial priesthood. "It is within the Church's mystery, as a mystery of Trinitarian communion in missionary tension, that every Christian identity is revealed, and likewise the specific identity of the priest and his ministry. Indeed, the priest, by virtue of the consecration which he receives in the Sacrament of Orders, is sent forth by the Father through the mediatorship of Jesus Christ, to whom he is configured in a special way as Head and Shepherd of his people, in order to live and work by the power of the Holy Spirit in service of the Church and for the salvation of the world. . . . Consequently, the nature and mission of the ministerial priesthood cannot be defined except through this multiple and rich interconnection of relationships which arise from the Blessed Trinity and are prolonged in the communion of the Church, as a sign and instrument of Christ, of communion with God and of the unity of all humanity" (*Pastores dabo vobis*, no. 12).

CHRISTOLOGICAL FOUNDATIONS

16.   The ministerial priesthood relies on Christological foundations. "Priests are called to prolong the presence of Christ, the One High Priest, embodying his way of life and making him visible in the midst of the flock entrusted to their care. . . . In the Church and on behalf of the Church, priests are a sacramental representation of Jesus Christ, the Head and Shepherd, authoritatively proclaiming his Word, repeating his acts of forgiveness and his offer of salvation, particularly in Baptism, Penance, and the Eucharist, showing his loving concern to the point of a total gift of self for the flock, which they gather into unity and lead to the Father through Christ and in the Spirit. In a word, priests exist and act in order to proclaim the Gospel to the world and to build up the Church in the name and person of Christ the Head and Shepherd" (*Pastores dabo vobis*, no. 15). Configured to Christ, Head and Shepherd of the Church, and intimately united as co-workers of the bishops, priests are commissioned in a unique way to continue Christ's mission as prophet, priest, and king.[11]

ECCLESIOLOGICAL FOUNDATIONS

17.   Finally, the ministerial priesthood has ecclesiological foundations. "The priesthood, along with the word of God and the sacramental signs which it serves, belongs to the constitutive elements of the Church. The ministry of the priest is entirely on behalf of the Church; it aims at promoting the exercise of the common priesthood of the entire people of God" (*Pastores dabo vobis*, no. 16). The priest's specific configuration to Christ also brings about this special relationship to his Body, the Church. His participation in Christ's priesthood is called "ministerial," for service to the members of the Body. Within the Body, "he represents Christ the Head, Shepherd, and Spouse of the Church" (*Pastores dabo vobis*, no. 16). *Pastores dabo vobis* expands the ecclesial foundation and sense of the ministerial priesthood, saying that it "is ordered not only to the particular Church but also to the universal Church, in communion with the Bishop, with Peter and under Peter. Through the priesthood of the Bishop, the priesthood of the second order is incorporated in the apostolic structure of the Church (cf. 2 Cor 5:20). In this way priests, like the Apostles, act as ambassadors

---

11   See *Rites of Ordination of a Bishop, of Priests, and of Deacons, Second Typical Edition* (Washington, DC: United States Conference of Catholic Bishops, 2003), nos. 101-102.

of Christ. This is the basis of the missionary character of every priest" (*Pastores dabo vobis*, no. 16).

PRIESTHOOD IN PRESBYTERAL COMMUNION

18.   The Trinitarian, Christological, and ecclesiological foundations give us a sense of the nature, mission, and ministry of priests. It is important, however, to add that these foundations only become real and operative in a presbyterate in communion with its bishop. "By its very nature, the ordained ministry can be carried out only to the extent that the priest is united to Christ through sacramental participation in the priestly order, and thus to the extent that he is in hierarchical communion with his own Bishop. The ordained ministry has a radical '*communitarian form*' and can only be carried out as a 'collective work'" (*Pastores dabo vobis*, no. 17). This "communitarian form" also means that priests ought to develop and foster bonds of fraternity and cooperation among themselves, so that the reality of the presbyterate may take hold of their lives.[12]

PRIESTHOOD: DIOCESAN AND RELIGIOUS

19.   Priestly ministry, whether lived out in a diocesan or religious life context, can appear to be very different: one more geographically and parish-bound, the other wider-ranging and rooted in a religious family's particular charism. Still, both diocesan and religious priests share a common ministerial priesthood, belong to a presbyterate in communion with a bishop, and serve the same mission of the Church. A common sacramental bond links both diocesan and religious priests, although particular circumstances of ministry and life may be diverse. It is, therefore, essential for all priests and those in priestly formation—both diocesan and religious—to understand and to see themselves as engaged in the Church's ministry subject to the same formation laid out in this *Program of Priestly Formation*.[13]

---

12   Second Vatican Council, *Presbyterorum ordinis* (*Decree on the Ministry and Life of Priests*) (1965), no. 8, in *Vatican Council II: The Conciliar and Post Conciliar Documents*, new revised edition, ed. Austin Flannery, OP (Northport, NY: Costello Publishing, 1996). All subsequent Vatican passages come from the Flannery edition.

13   This means not only that diocesan priests form a presbyterate, but that "religious clergy who live and work in a particular Church also belong to the one presbyterate, albeit under a different title" (*Pastores dabo vobis*, no. 74).

The Life of Priests

20.   When the Second Vatican Council's *Decree on the Ministry and Life of Priests* (*Presbyterorum ordinis*) speaks of "the life of priests," it refers to the whole of their existence but especially to the spiritual dimension that is at the center of all life. In today's context of fragmentation, it is especially important to note and hold fast to "the one necessary thing" (see Lk 10:42).

21.   Along with all the baptized who have been claimed for new life in Christ by the power of the Holy Spirit, priests are called with their brothers and sisters to live out their baptismal call as disciples of Jesus Christ and to grow in holiness.[14]

22.   At the same time, priests are called to a specific vocation to holiness in virtue of their new consecration in the sacrament of Holy Orders, a consecration that configures them to Christ the Head and Shepherd (*Pastores dabo vobis*, no. 20). This configuration to Christ endows the priest with the mission and ministry, which is specific to him and which obliges him to be a "living instrument of Christ the eternal priest" and to act "in the name and in the person of Christ himself" and with his entire "life," called to witness in a fundamental way to the "radicalism of the Gospel."[15]

23.   For priests, the specific arena in which their spiritual life unfolds is their exercise of ministry in fulfillment of their mission.[16] The life of priests in the Spirit means their continuous transformation and conversion of heart centered on the integration or linking of their identity as configured to Christ, Head and Shepherd (*Pastores dabo vobis*, nos. 21-23), with their ministry of word, sacrament, and pastoral governance or leadership (*Pastores dabo vobis*, nos. 24-26).

---

14   See Second Vatican Council, *Lumen gentium* (*Dogmatic Constitution on the Church*) (1964), nos. 39-42; *Pastores dabo vobis*, no. 20.

15   See *Pastores dabo vobis*, no. 20.

16   See *Pastores dabo vobis*, no. 24; *Presbyterorum ordinis*, no. 12; Synod of Bishops, *The Ministerial Priesthood and Justice in the World* (1971), part 2, I, iii.

24.   The ministry itself, by which the priest brings Christ's redemptive gifts to his people, transforms the priest's own life. In a particular way, the celebrations of Baptism, Penance, and the Eucharist lead the priest to a holy encounter with God's all-transforming, merciful love.

25.   When the priest's identity as configured to Christ culminates in his ministry on behalf of Christ, which is called *amoris officium* (a work of love), he finds his unity of life in pastoral charity. *Presbyterorum ordinis*, no. 14, says: "Priests will achieve the unity of their lives by joining themselves with Christ in the recognition of the Father's will and in the gift of themselves to the flock entrusted to them. In this way, by adopting the role of the good shepherd they will find in the practice of pastoral charity itself the bond of priestly perfection which will reduce to unity their life and activity."

26.   Priestly life lived in configuration to Jesus Christ, Head and Shepherd, must necessarily manifest and give witness to the radicalism of the Gospel. In other words, priests are called to a way of life that gives evident and transparent witness to the power of the Gospel at work in their lives. The elements of such a lifestyle—named here and to be developed elsewhere in the PPF—include

- A way of life permeated by the three-fold charge given priests at ordination to teach, to sanctify, and to govern[17]
- A life of steady prayer first and foremost centered in the sacraments, especially in the Eucharist (see *Ecclesia de Eucharistia*, no. 31), the Liturgy of the Hours, and the liturgical cycles, but also in prayer that is personal and devotional (see *Pastores dabo vobis*, no. 33)
- A deep devotion to the person of Jesus Christ, Son of God and Son of Mary, Lord and Savior (see *Pastores dabo vobis*, no. 46)
- A life of obedience that is apostolic, communal, and pastoral (see *Pastores dabo vobis*, no. 28)
- A life lived in communion with one's bishop and the presbyterate, a communion that includes sacramental, apostolic, and fraternal bonds[18]

---

[17]   See *Presbyterorum ordinis*, nos. 4-6, 13; *Pastores dabo vobis*, no. 26; Second Vatican Council, *Optatam totius* (*Decree on the Training of Priests*) (1965), no. 21.

[18]   See *Rites of Ordination of a Bishop, of Priests, and of Deacons*, no. 101; *Presbyterorum ordinis*, nos. 7-8, 14; *Pastores dabo vobis*, no. 17.

- For religious priests, a life in community with one's fellow religious in accord with the institute's rule of life
- A life of celibate chastity that serves as both "a sign and stimulus of love, and as a singular source of spiritual fertility in the world"[19] and, being freely accepted, shows that the priest is "consecrated in a new way to Christ"[20] and offers in himself a reflection of the virginal love of Christ for the Church[21]
- A life of gratitude for the material blessings of God's creation coupled with a simple and generous lifestyle that cares for and is in solidarity with the poor, works for universal justice, makes itself ready and available for all those in need, administers the goods of the community with utmost honesty, and offers a courageous prophetic witness in the world[22]
- A life that embraces "the mind and heart of missionaries open to the needs of the Church and the world"[23]
- A life that promotes the array of ecclesial vocations

27.   Although the life of vowed religious priests encompasses everything that has been said about the life of priests generally, the experience and the exercise of the ministerial priesthood within the context of religious life differs from that of the diocesan priesthood.

28.   The primary context of religious priesthood ordinarily comes from the nature of religious life itself. Religious who are called to priesthood exercise that ministry within the context of their religious charism. The exercise of priesthood takes on a distinctive quality for a religious, depending upon the rule of life and the charism of a particular institute or society.

29.   To a great extent, the deeper identification of religious with the charism of their founders today is due to their obedience to the directives of the Second Vatican Council. "The up-to-date renewal of the religious life comprises both a constant return to the sources of the whole of the

---

19   Lumen gentium, no. 42. See Presbyterorum ordinis, no. 16; Rites of Ordination of a Bishop, of Priests, and of Deacons, no. 199.
20   Rites of Ordination of a Bishop, of Priests, and of Deacons, no. 177.
21   See Second Vatican Council, Sacrosanctum concilium (Constitution on the Sacred Liturgy) (1963), no. 26; Presbyterorum ordinis, no. 16.
22   See Pastores dabo vobis, no. 30.
23   Pastores dabo vobis, no. 32, citing John Paul II, Redemptoris missio (On the Permanent Validity of the Church's Missionary Mandate) (1990), no. 67. See Redemptoris missio, nos. 15-16.

Christian life and to the primitive inspiration of the institutes, and their adaptation to the changed conditions of our time."[24]

30.   Centuries of tradition bear witness to a difference between formation for religious life and formation of candidates for the priesthood. Formation for religious life must always take into account the charism, history, and mission of the particular institute or society, while recognizing the human, spiritual, intellectual, and pastoral requirements incumbent upon all who are called to the ministerial priesthood.

31.   This program outlines the requirements shared by religious and diocesan candidates for priesthood while recognizing the different process of spiritual formation incumbent upon those whose primary call is to be of service to the Church through religious life and for whom fidelity to the charism of their founder is the gift that is shared.[25]

---

24   Second Vatican Council, *Perfectae caritatis* (*Decree on the Adaptation and Renewal of Religious Life*) (1965), no. 2.

25   See Sacred Congregation for Religious and for Secular Institutes/Sacred Congregation for Bishops, *Mutuae relationes* (*Mutual Relations*) (1978); Congregation for Institutes of Consecrated Life and Societies of Apostolic Life, *Directives on Formation in Religious Institutes* (1990).

Priestly Vocations in the Church's Pastoral Work and the Admission of Candidates

VARIOUS RESPONSIBILITIES IN THE CHURCH FOR VOCATIONS

32.   The whole Church receives the gift of vocations from God and is responsible for promoting and discerning vocations.[26] The entire Church is to be engaged in the pastoral work of promoting vocations.[27] It is integral to the mission of the Church "to care for the birth, discernment, and fostering of vocations, particularly those to the priesthood."[28] Within that ecclesial context, there are various responsibilities:

- *The Church*: The whole Church through prayer, active cooperation, and the witness of living full Christian lives takes responsibility for vocations.[29]
- *The family*: "A very special responsibility falls upon the *Christian family*, which by virtue of the Sacrament of Matrimony shares in its own unique way in the educational mission of the Church, Teacher, and Mother." Families can become "a first seminary in which children can acquire from the beginning an awareness of piety and prayer and of love for the Church" (*Pastores dabo vobis*, no. 41).
- *The bishop*: "The first responsibility for the pastoral work of promoting priestly vocations lies with the *Bishop*, who is called to be the first to exercise this responsibility, even though he can and must call upon many others to cooperate with him" (*Pastores dabo*

---

26   See *Pastores dabo vobis*, nos. 34-41; CIC, c. 233.
27   See CIC, c. 233§1.
28   *Pastores dabo vobis*, no. 34.
29   See *Pastores dabo vobis*, no. 41.

vobis, no. 41). However he shares his responsibility, the pastoral task of promoting priestly vocations remains his task for which he must continue to offer supervision and direct involvement.[30] As the one responsible for the unity of the local church and its communion with the universal Church, the bishop, especially in the context of the United States, must encourage a wide range of candidates who represent the cultural and linguistic diversity of his diocese.

- *The presbyterate*: "The Bishop can rely above all on the cooperation of his presbyterate. All its *priests* are united to him and share his responsibility in seeking and fostering priestly vocations" (*Pastores dabo vobis*, no. 41). They do this by inviting men to consider the priesthood as a possible vocation. For those who are discerning the call, priests can nurture their sense of vocation and be invaluable mentors along the path of discernment. Through their priestly ministry, especially in parish assignments, priests are able to recognize the prayerfulness, the talents, and the character of men who may be called to priestly ministry. "At the same time the diligence of priests in carrying out their Eucharistic ministry, together with the conscious, active, and fruitful participation of the faithful in the Eucharist, provides young men with a powerful example and incentive for responding generously to God's call. Often it is the example of a priest's fervent charity which the Lord uses to sow and to bring to fruition in a young man's heart the seed of a priestly calling."[31]

- *The vocation director*: In dioceses and religious institutes in the United States, generally there is a vocation director (or team) who serves on behalf of the bishop and presbyterate or the religious ordinary and institute or society to promote vocations (the work of *recruitment*) and to direct those vocations while in discernment (the work of *supervision* or *direction*). In his supervisory function, a diocesan vocation director may manage the diocesan process of the admission of candidates, serve as a liaison between the diocesan bishop and the seminary, and link the seminarian-candidates to the diocese and presbyterate, e.g., through the placement of interns. He collaborates with the bishop, with the presbyter-

---

30   See CIC, c. 385.
31   John Paul II, *Ecclesia de Eucharistia* (*On the Eucharist*) (Washington, DC: United States Conference of Catholic Bishops, 2003), no. 31.

ate, with a diocesan vocation commission if one is in place, and with the seminary. A religious vocation director's role may vary according to the division of labor in a given religious institute or society. In all cases, the relationship with the seminary merits special attention. Mutual respect and collaboration should mark the relation of vocation and seminary personnel. Each possesses different responsibilities; yet cooperation, mutual knowledge, and trust are vital for the good of the candidates and the benefit of the Church. Such collaboration is especially important concerning the recommendation of applicants for admission and their continuing evaluation. Visitations to the seminary on the part of the bishop, religious ordinary, and vocation personnel should be encouraged.[32] The bishop's own relationship with the seminary and his seminarians should never be simply left to the seminary or vocations personnel. Often it may be helpful for seminary faculty to visit the local dioceses and religious communities they serve.

- *The seminary*: The seminary plays a collaborative role in the promotion and an important role in the discernment of vocations. A seminary attached to a particular diocese often subsumes the responsibilities of a diocesan vocation director/recruiter. In the seminary, the rector, assisted by his faculty, is especially important in promoting, assessing, and developing priestly vocations. His leadership in this role is spiritual, pastoral, and administrative.

- *Seminarians*: Seminarians also play a significant role in promoting priestly vocations through the friendships they form outside the seminary setting, through their visible presence in their home parishes, through their involvement in Christian service activities and field education, through their assistance with vocation programs, and through the welcome they extend to visitors at the seminary.

THE DISCERNMENT OF VOCATIONS

33. Potential candidates for the priesthood must be in prayerful dialogue with God and with the Church in the discernment of their vocation. The linkage of this divine and ecclesial dialogue is especially important because "in the present context there is . . . a certain tendency

---

32 See CIC, cc. 396-397, 628.

to view the bond between human beings and God in an individualistic and self-centered way, as if God's call reached the individual by a direct route, without in any way passing through the community" (*Pastores dabo vobis*, no. 37). Eventually, this dialogue, properly conducted, may bring candidates to the admissions process, completing this first phase of vocational discernment.

THE ADMISSIONS PROCESS

34.   The purpose of the admissions process is to determine whether candidates have the requisite qualities to begin the process of formation and preparation for priestly ordination and ministry. In a global way, *Pastores dabo vobis* offers these criteria as a basis for admission to the seminary program: "a right intention, . . . a sufficiently broad knowledge of the doctrine of the faith, some introduction to the methods of prayer, and behavior in conformity with Christian tradition. They should also have attitudes proper to their regions, through which they can express their effort to find God and the faith" (*Pastores dabo vobis*, no. 62).

35.   In forming a prudent judgment about the suitability of an applicant for priestly formation, the principle of gradualism should be used. According to the principle of gradualism, progressively higher levels of expectations should be sought as an applicant seeks admission to progressively higher levels of preparation, moving from the preparatory to the collegiate or pre-theologate, and finally to the theologate program. In short, the closer the program is to priestly ordination, the greater the applicant's development of the requisite qualities ought to be. The principle of gradualism recognizes that it would be unrealistic to expect an applicant for admission to be fully mature in all areas.

36.   The principle of gradualism, however, does not deny that a minimal level of development is necessary for admission to any level of priestly formation. The minimal qualities necessary for admission are properly understood as *thresholds* or *foundations*. All applicants need to have passed through certain thresholds of human, spiritual, intellectual, and pastoral development, which will serve as foundations for further development. For example, if a candidate has achieved a threshold of a basic capacity for empathy and communication, he would seem to have a foundation upon which pastoral formation could develop.

37.   Candidates for admission, in other words, should have attained, at least in some measure, growth in those areas represented by the four pillars or in the integrated dimensions of formation identified in *Pastores dabo vobis*: human, spiritual, intellectual, and pastoral. In trying to determine what is *sufficient* growth or development in these areas, seminaries ought to be clear and specific. For example, sufficient human formation for admission means not only an absence of serious pathology but also a proven capacity to function competently in ordinary human situations without need to do extensive therapeutic or remedial work to be fully functioning, a psychosexual maturity commensurate with chronological age, a genuine empathy that enables the applicant to connect well and personally with others, a capacity for growth or conversion, and a deep desire to be a man for others in the likeness of Christ. Sufficient spiritual formation means a well catechized person who prays daily, belongs to a parish, participates at least weekly in the Sunday Eucharist and regularly in the Sacrament of Penance, and is drawn to explore and deepen his spiritual life and share it with others. Sufficient intellectual formation means proven capacities for critical thinking, an ability to understand both abstract and practical questions, and the capacity to understand other persons and to communicate effectively with them in both oral and written form. Sufficient pastoral formation means having a fundamental sense of the Church's mission and a generous willingness and enthusiasm to promote it and knowing how the ordained priesthood contributes to the mission; having a sensitivity to the needs of others and a desire to respond to them; and having a willingness to initiate action and assume a position of leadership for the good of individuals and communities. Finally, candidates should also have the *right intention* when they present themselves for admission to the seminary. Their intention to pursue preparation for priestly ordination and ministry ought to correspond to the Church's understanding.

38.   In contrast to previous generations, when a more homogenous population presented itself for entrance to the seminary, today's candidates represent a considerable diversity—not only of differing personal gifts and levels of maturity but also significant cultural differences—that must be taken into account. All those involved in the evaluation of applicants for priestly formation must appreciate cultural, generational, educational, and familial differences and be able to recognize which are gifts, which are liabilities, and which are simply indications of a need for fuller growth.

39.   At the diocesan level, the primary responsibility for overseeing the admissions process belongs to the bishop. Ultimately, of course, it is the responsibility of the bishop or religious ordinary to decide whether or not to admit candidates to priestly formation, in accordance with the criteria which have been properly established.[33] The bishop or religious ordinary shares his responsibility with the vocation director or vocation team, perhaps also with a vocation board or commission, and with the local parishes. The admissions process requires sacramental records, autobiography, a review of the psychological and medical assessment (with due regard for CIC, c. 241, and *Ratio fundamentalis*, no. 39), observations of the potential candidates during the course of their visits to the seminary, interviews, transcripts, criminal background checks, and immigration documentation as well as letters of reference.[34] Bishops, religious superiors, and rectors must have moral certitude about the psychological and physical health of those they admit to the seminary. In particular, they should be assured that applicants have a requisite level of affective maturity and the capacity to live celibate chastity. They will determine the means necessary to arrive at such certitude, including, for example, their own interviews with applicants, the reliable testimony of those who have known the applicants, and psychological and physical assessments made by expert consultants. Whenever possible, the diocese and the seminary should conduct separate admission procedures to ensure the broadest and most objective screening possible, while avoiding a duplication of these efforts.

40.   Although this process aims primarily at determining the fitness of an applicant for a seminary program, once an applicant is admitted to a seminary program, the results of the process contribute to the seminarian's personal agenda for priestly formation. Specifically, the observations and conclusions that emerge from the admissions process should serve as a significant resource for the seminarian's human, spiritual, intellectual, and pastoral formation within the seminary. The sharing of this information presumes a due respect for the rights of the seminarian and a prudent maintenance of confidentiality.

41.   Without denying the importance of evaluating minimal thresholds in all areas of an applicant's development, high standards and strict

---

33   See CIC, c. 241§1; CCEO, c. 342§1.
34   See CIC, c. 241§2; CCEO, c. 342§2.

vigilance are especially necessary in evaluating human thresholds pertaining to sexuality. "*Sexuality* affects all aspects of the human person in the unity of his body and soul. It especially concerns affectivity, the capacity to love and to procreate, and in a more general way the attitude for forming bonds of communion with others."[35] For the seminary applicant, thresholds pertaining to sexuality serve as the foundation for living a lifelong commitment to healthy, chaste celibacy. As we have recently seen so dramatically in the Church, when such foundations are lacking in priests, the consequent suffering and scandals are devastating.

NORMS FOR THE ADMISSION OF CANDIDATES

42.   Seminaries as well as dioceses must have clear written statements of admission policies, which are to be regularly reviewed and updated. These policies include behavioral criteria which place the burden of qualification for admission to the seminary on applicants. In cases in which the admission committee has reservations, caution should be taken and the benefit of the doubt given to the Church. It is also important that the admission procedure carefully weigh the potential impact of the admission of each individual on the whole seminary community.

43.   Seminaries should specify *thresholds* or *foundations* in a way that permits those charged with admitting candidates to have clear criteria available. This approach to admissions assumes that the seminary formation program is not the place for long term therapy or remedial work, which should be completed prior to a decision concerning admission.

44.   Applicants must give evidence of an overall personal balance, good moral character, a love for the truth, and proper motivation. This includes the requisite human, moral, spiritual, intellectual, physical, and psychological qualities for priestly ministry.[36]

---

35   *Catechism of the Catholic Church* (CCC), 2nd ed. (Washington, DC: Libreria Editrice Vaticana–United States Conference of Catholic Bishops, 2000), no. 2332. Some subsequent citations appear in the text.

36   See CIC, c. 241§1; CCEO, c. 342§1.

45. All applicants should give witness to their conviction that God has brought them to the seminary to discern whether or not they are really called to the priesthood, and they should commit themselves wholeheartedly to carrying out that discernment. They should be alert both to signs that seem to confirm that call and to counter-indications. As a seminarian moves from a high school seminary program to college seminary to the theologate, there should be a growing sense of confirmation of that call.

46. Applicants for pre-theology must follow a careful and thorough admissions process equivalent to entrance procedures for the theologate. This process may result in specific recommendations concerning the applicant's program.

47. Applicants must undergo a thorough screening process. Personal interviews with the applicants, evaluations from their pastors and teachers, records and evaluations from a previous seminary or religious community if applicable, academic records, standardized test scores, psychological evaluations, and criminal background checks are all components of an effective admission program and are weighed together with an assessment of the applicant's motivation. Those who do not fulfill these entrance requirements of the seminary must not be admitted.

48. It is the responsibility of the vocation director (or representative of the religious community) to provide the seminary in a timely and complete fashion the results of the screening process used by the diocese or religious community.

49. Applicants from diverse ethnic and cultural backgrounds should be given every encouragement. Seminaries are responsible to ensure the possession of adequate resources to serve the formative needs of such applicants. Academic requirements should not be lessened, but necessary adaptations may be made to enable admission into the regular course of study. Applicants must have an adequate command of the English language to begin intellectual formation in a seminary in which English is the language of instruction. English language studies may be undertaken in the seminary before admission into the full, regular courses of seminary study. It is also important that applicants from other countries receive special help in gaining the necessary understanding of the religious and cultural context for priestly ministry and life in the United States.

50.   Theologates must require a bachelor's degree or its equivalent from an accredited institution. Sufficient education in philosophy, which the *Code of Canon Law* states as a biennium,[37] is understood in the United States to be at least 30 semester credit hours, plus the out-of-classroom work associated with each credit hour traditionally expected in American higher education. A minimum of 12 semester credit hours is required in appropriate courses of undergraduate theology. (The content of such courses is outlined in norms 178 and 179 under "Intellectual Formation—College Seminaries: Norms.")

51.   Seminaries should draw up guidelines for psychologists and admission personnel and describe those human traits and qualities that are consonant with an authentic vocation to the priesthood as well as those counter-indications that would suggest that the applicant is not a suitable candidate. Seminaries as well as dioceses and religious communities must be assured that those who conduct psychological evaluations for them are well versed in and supportive of the Church's expectations of candidates for the priesthood, especially expectations concerning celibacy and permanence of commitment.

52.   A psychological assessment is an integral part of the admission procedure. Psychological assessments should be administered using methods that do not violate the applicant's right to privacy and confidentiality or do harm to the reputation of the applicant.[38] At the same time, the applicant should understand that the testing results will be shared with select seminary personnel in a way that permits a thorough review. Due care should be observed in correctly interpreting the results of psychological testing in light of the cultural background of applicants.

53.   The admissions process ought to give sufficient attention to the emotional health of applicants. Special care and scrutiny should be given to those who manifest dysfunction or come from dysfunctional families. It is possible for some seminarians to address these issues in the course of a seminary program through counseling or other means. Their willingness, however, to confront these or other personal issues should be determined prior to the decision about admission. If long-term therapeutic work is indicated, this is best accomplished before the decision is made concerning

---

37   See CIC, c. 250; CCEO, c. 348; *Pastores dabo vobis*, no. 56.
38   See CIC, c. 220; CCEO, c. 23.

entrance into the seminary. At times, the gravity of family or personal issues is such that, if the candidate has not yet adequately dealt with these issues, entrance into the seminary program should be denied.

54.   The admissions procedure should include an open and frank discussion of the life experiences that applicants bring to the seminary. Their level of insight or self-knowledge and their willingness to address important human issues, such as their interpersonal abilities, evidence of sound peer relationships, their manner of dealing with authority, and their psychosexual development, can be important gauges of their readiness to enter a seminary program. If the applicant is unaware of or unresolved concerning significant human issues, the seminary is well advised to delay admission until greater clarity or resolution is evident. Concerning the capacity to live the charism of celibacy, the applicant should give evidence of having lived in continence for a sustained period of time, which would be for at least two years before entering a priestly formation program.

55.   Any evidence of criminal sexual activity with a minor or an inclination toward such activity disqualifies the applicant from admission.[39]

56.   With regard to the admission of candidates with same-sex experiences and/or inclinations, the guidelines provided by the Holy See must be followed.

57.   Concerning the results of psychological testing and other confidential materials, the seminary must observe all legal requirements, inform the applicant in writing of his specific rights to privacy and confidentiality, and utilize appropriate release forms.[40] Throughout the admission process and, if accepted, after entrance into the seminary, the candidate's right to privacy should be respected and the careful management of confidential materials is to be observed. This is especially true in the case of sharing confidential information with a team of formators, while at the same time ensuring that those charged with the candidate's growth and integration have the clear and specific information they need so that they can help the candidate achieve the growth necessary to become a "man of

---

39   See *Essential Norms for Diocesan/Eparchial Policies Dealing with Allegations of Sexual Abuse of Minors by Priests or Deacons* (Washington, DC: United States Conference of Catholic Bishops, 2006), http://www.nccbuscc.org/ocyp/2005EssentialNorms.pdf.

40   See CIC, c. 220; CCEO, c. 23.

communion."[41] The rector must observe a careful vigilance that protects the privacy and reputation of the seminarian in his relationship with the formation faculty. The traditional distinction between internal and external forum is to be maintained. Clear policies must be enunciated concerning who may have access to any of the admissions materials. Clear directives must be in place to determine any further use of psychological testing results or other admissions materials for formation or even counseling purposes.

58.   In the admissions process, an evaluation should be made of a candidate's indebtedness, his ability to handle finances (i.e., responsible record-keeping and payment of personal taxes), spending patterns, and a willingness to cover a portion of his seminary expenses. Candidates should demonstrate an aptitude for learning principles of good stewardship, avoiding any attitudes of entitlement. They should also show an openness to developing professional approaches to personal and church-related business matters.

59.   The admissions process should be attentive to older, experienced applicants, who often bring a mature spirituality, experience in pastoral life, and other significant life experiences, but who might also be less susceptible to formation. The seminary admissions process must be no less rigorous, thorough, or comprehensive than it might be for other applicants.

60.   Diocesan bishops, religious ordinaries, vocation directors, and seminaries should recognize that additional time will be necessary to prepare candidates without previous seminary formation for entrance into the theologate. If a person has no previous preparation in a formation program, then the pre-theology program should extend over a two-year calendar period. Pre-theology programs are designed to address all four pillars of formation, not simply to meet academic requirements.

61.   If applicants have been in a seminary or formation program previously, dioceses, religious institutes or societies, and seminaries must consult all previous institutions about the past record of these applicants as

---

41   "Of special importance is the capacity to relate to others. This is truly fundamental for a person who is called to be responsible for a community and to be a 'man of communion.' This demands that the priest not be arrogant or quarrelsome, but affable, hospitable, sincere in his words and heart, prudent and discreet, generous and ready to serve, capable of opening himself to clear and brotherly relationships and of encouraging the same in others and quick to understand, forgive, and console" (*Pastores dabo vobis*, no. 43).

prescribed in the *Norms Concerning Applications for Priestly Formation from Those Previously Enrolled in a Formation Program.*[42] If such records indicate difficulties, before admitting the applicant, the seminary should proceed cautiously and ascertain whether problems have been resolved and sufficient positive growth has taken place.

62.   If an applicant has been dismissed from a program of priestly formation or from an institute of consecrated life or society of apostolic life, no subsequent application will be considered in the two years following such dismissal. If the departure was other than a dismissal, sufficient time should be allotted to evaluate carefully his application and background. (See Addendum A.)

63.   Prior to admission, the diocese or religious community is obliged to ensure (and the seminary must verify) that recent Baptism and Confirmation certificates (CIC, c. 241§2, 1050, 1033; CCEO, c. 342§2, 769§1, 1°) have been obtained. Although a valid marriage certificate of the applicant's parents is no longer canonically required, the seminary may request it to gain further insight into the applicant's family background. The diocese must also obtain the following documentation from others: summaries of personal interviews with the applicant, evaluation from his pastor and teachers, academic records, standardized test scores, assessments by experienced formators of the applicant's motivation, and, if applicable, previous seminary evaluations. The seminary must verify the completion of all documentation before a candidate is admitted.

64.   The seminary is also obligated to determine the freedom of the applicant from impediments to orders and from conditions that must be addressed prior to the reception of orders, namely: that sufficient time has passed for a neophyte (CIC, c. 1042, 3°; CCEO, c. 762§1, 8°); that the applicant does not hold a position forbidden to clerics (CIC, cc. 285-286, 289, 1042 2° and 3°; CCEO, cc. 762§1, 7° and 8°, 382-385); that the applicant does not "labor under some form of insanity or psychic defect" (CIC, c. 1041 1° and 2°; CCEO, cc. 172§1,1°, 762§1, 1° and 2°); that he has not committed apostasy, heresy, or schism (CIC, c. 1041, 2°; CCEO, c. 762§1, 2°); that he has not committed homicide, cooperated in an abortion (CIC, c. 1041, 4°; CCEO, c. 762§1, 4°), mutilated himself or another, attempted suicide (CIC, c. 1041, 5°; CCEO, c. 762§1, 5°), or simulated

---

42   See *Norms Concerning Applications for Priestly Formation from Those Previously Enrolled in a Formation Program* in Addendum A; CIC, c. 241§3; CCEO, c. 342§3.

an act reserved to priests or bishops (CIC, c. 1041, 6°; CCEO, c. 762§1, 6°). If any of these conditions exist, then prior to admission, appropriate dispensations or remedies must be obtained. It is also recommended that the seminary investigate whether the candidate is allergic to wheat, whether he is able to consume the Precious Blood, whether he is abusing alcohol or drugs, whether he has a criminal background, whether he has ever been sexually abused as a minor, and whether any remedies would be appropriate.

65.   The admission process by the diocese or religious community must include a thorough physical examination to ensure that applicants possess the good health necessary for seminary training and priestly ministry. This exam should include HIV and drug testing.

66.   An applicant for the priesthood must testify that he is not married or, if he is married, he has the approval of the Holy See. If an Eastern Catholic candidate is married, a certificate of marriage is required along with the written consent of his wife (CCEO, c. 769§1, 2°) and the approval of the Apostolic See. Applicants who have received a declaration of matrimonial nullity should be carefully screened. Although these men may have canonical freedom to pursue the priesthood, it is important to ascertain if and how previous obstacles to a marriage commitment or possible scandal might affect their viability as candidates for the priesthood. Care must be taken to certify the canonical declaration of nullity by reviewing the *Acta* (official documentation and evidence for the canonical decision) to ensure that the reasons and circumstances that serve as warrants for the declaration of nullity are fully disclosed to the sponsoring bishop or religious ordinary, rector, and the seminary admissions committee. If a previously married person has responsibilities for his spouse, this factor is to be considered. If the candidate has responsibility for a minor child, acceptance should be deferred. All such cases should be carefully weighed.

67.   Especially careful screening should also be given to applicants who are recent converts to the Catholic faith or who have lapsed in the practice of their faith and have recently returned. It is advisable that at least two years pass between their entry into the Church and their acceptance into a seminary program. A suitable period of time should pass before entrance into the seminary in cases of Catholics for whom a sudden conversion experience seems to precipitate a priestly vocation. Similarly, those who return to the practice of the faith after an extended period away from the Church should not enter the seminary directly.

The Formation of
Candidates for Priesthood

68.   Formation, as the Church understands it, is not equivalent to a secular sense of schooling or, even less, job training. Formation is first and foremost cooperation with the grace of God. In the United States Conference of Catholic Bishops' document *The Basic Plan for the Ongoing Formation of Priests*, a reflection on St. Paul's words in 2 Corinthians 3:17-18 leads to a description of formation. "The apostle Paul marvels at the work of the Holy Spirit who transforms believers into the very image of Jesus Christ, who himself is the image of God. This grace of the new covenant embraces all who have joined themselves to Jesus Christ in faith and baptism. Indeed, it is sheer grace, all God's doing. Moved by that grace, however, we make ourselves available to God's work of transformation. And that making ready a place for the Lord to dwell in us and transform us we call formation."[43]

69.   All priestly formation takes place within the context of the Church as the Body of Christ and in relationship to the mission of the Church. Thus it is essential that the formation of the candidate for priesthood be integrated within the wider ecclesial dimension so that the candidate understands his role as a priest to be the representative and servant of the Church.

70.   The seminary and its programs foster the formation of future priests by attending specifically to their human, spiritual, intellectual, and pastoral formation—the four pillars of priestly formation developed in *Pastores dabo vobis*. These pillars of formation and their finality give specificity to formation in seminaries as well as a sense of the integrated wholeness of the different dimensions of formation. "Although this formation [in seminaries] has many aspects in common with the human and Christian formation of all the members of the Church, it has, neverthe-

---

43   United States Conference of Catholic Bishops, *The Basic Plan for the Ongoing Formation of Priests*, (Washington, DC: United States Conference of Catholic Bishops, 2001), 7.

less, contents, modalities, and characteristics which relate specifically to the aim of preparation for the priesthood . . . the Seminary should have a precise *program*, a program of life characterized by its being organized and unified . . . with one aim which justifies the existence of the Seminary: preparation of future priests" (*Pastores dabo vobis*, no. 61).

71. The goal is the development not just of a well-rounded person, a prayerful person, or an experienced pastoral practitioner but rather one who understands his spiritual development within the context of his call to service in the Church, his human development within the greater context of his call to advance the mission of the Church, his intellectual development as the appropriation of the Church's teaching and tradition, and his pastoral formation as participation in the active ministry of the Church.

72. The sections that follow on human, spiritual, intellectual, and pastoral formation are to be read in this unified and integrated sense. These are neither discrete nor layered dimensions of priestly existence, but they are—as we shall see—interrelated aspects of a human response to God's transforming grace.

73. Clearly human formation is the foundation for the other three pillars. Spiritual formation informs the other three. Intellectual formation appropriates and understands the other three. Pastoral formation expresses the other three pillars in practice.

I. HUMAN FORMATION

74. The foundation and center of all human formation is Jesus Christ, the Word made flesh. In his fully developed humanity, he was truly free and with complete freedom gave himself totally for the salvation of the world.[44] *Pastores dabo vobis*, no. 5, expresses the Christological foundation of human formation: "The Letter to the Hebrews clearly affirms the '*human character*' of God's minister: he comes from the human community and is at its service, imitating Jesus Christ 'who in every respect has been tempted as we are, yet without sin' (Heb 4:15)."

---

44   See Jn 10:17-18; Mk 10:45.

75.   The basic principle of human formation is to be found in *Pastores dabo vobis*, no. 43: the human personality of the priest is to be a bridge and not an obstacle for others in their meeting with Jesus Christ the Redeemer of the human race. As the humanity of the Word made flesh was the *instrumentum salutis*, so the humanity of the priest is instrumental in mediating the redemptive gifts of Christ to people today.[45] As *Pastores dabo vobis* also emphasizes, human formation is the "necessary foundation" of priestly formation.

[handwritten margin note: Priest must meet people in thier HUMANITY]

76.   The human formation of candidates for the priesthood aims to prepare them to be apt instruments of Christ's grace. It does so by fostering the growth of a man who can be described in these ways:

- A *free person*: a person who is free *to be* who he is in God's design, someone who does not—in contrast to the popular culture—conceive or pursue freedom as the expansion of options or as individual autonomy detached from others[46]
- A *person of solid moral character with a finely developed moral conscience, a man open to and capable of conversion*: a man who demonstrates the human virtues of prudence, fortitude, temperance, justice, humility, constancy, sincerity, patience, good manners, truthfulness, and keeping his word, and who also manifests growth in the practice of these virtues
- A *prudent and discerning man*: someone who demonstrates a "capacity for critical observation so that [he] can discern true and false values, since this is an essential requirement for establishing a constructive dialogue with the world of today"[47]
- A *man of communion*: a person who has real and deep relational capacities, someone who can enter into genuine dialogue and friendship, a person of true empathy who can understand and know other persons, a person open to others and available to them with a generosity of spirit. The man of communion is capable of making a gift of himself and of receiving the gift of

---

45   From this foundation would stem those particular human qualities identified by Pope John Paul II in *Pastores dabo vobis*, no. 43: "These qualities are needed for them to be balanced people, strong and free, capable of bearing the weight of pastoral responsibilities. They need to be educated to love the truth, to be loyal, to respect every person, to have a sense of justice, to be true to their word, to be genuinely compassionate, to be men of integrity and, especially, to be balanced in judgment and behavior."

46   See John Paul II, *Veritatis splendor* (*The Splendor of Truth*) (1993), no. 34.

47   John Paul II, *Ecclesia in America* (*The Church in America*) (Washington, DC: United States Conference of Catholic Bishops, 1999), no. 40.

others. This, in fact, requires the full possession of oneself. This life should be one of inner joy and inner peace—signs of self-possession and generosity.

- A *good communicator*: someone who listens well, is articulate, and has the skills of effective communication, someone capable of public speaking

- A *person of affective maturity*: someone whose life of feelings is in balance and integrated into thought and values; in other words, a man of feelings who is not driven by them but freely lives his life enriched by them; this might be especially evidenced in his ability to live well with authority and in his ability to take direction from another, and to exercise authority well among his peers, as well as an ability to deal productively with conflict and stress

- A *man who respects, cares for, and has vigilance over his body*: a person who pays appropriate attention to his physical well-being, so that he has the energy and strength to accomplish the tasks entrusted to him and the self-knowledge to face temptation and resist it effectively

- A *man who relates well with others, free of overt prejudice and willing to work with people of diverse cultural backgrounds*: a man capable of wholesome relations with women and men as relatives, friends, colleagues, staff members, and teachers, and as encountered in areas of apostolic work

- A *good steward of material possessions*: someone who is able to live a simple style of life and able to "avoid whatever has a semblance of vanity";[48] someone who has the right attitude toward the goods of this world, since his "portion and inheritance" is the Lord;[49] someone who is generous in making charitable contributions and sustaining the poor[50]

- A *man who can take on the role of a public person*: someone both secure in himself and convinced of his responsibility who is able to live not just as a private citizen but as a public person in service of the Gospel and representing the Church

---

48   CIC, c. 282; CCEO, c. 385§1.
49   Ps 16:5-6.
50   See *Presbyterorum ordinis*, no. 17.

77.   Human formation comes together in a particular way in the domain of human sexuality, and this is especially true for those who are preparing for a life of celibacy. The various dimensions of being a human person—the physical, the psychological, and the spiritual—converge in affective maturity, which includes human sexuality. Education is necessary for understanding sexuality and living chastely. Those preparing to live out a celibate commitment face particular challenges, especially in today's cultural context of permissiveness. *# Masorlindr*

78.   Education for chastity, a virtue incumbent on all Christians and in a unique way embraced in celibacy, ought to present it as a "virtue that develops a person's authentic maturity and makes him or her capable of respecting and fostering the 'nuptial meaning' of the body" (*Pastores dabo vobis*, no. 44). For all Christians, whatever their state of life, chastity cultivates the capacity for authentic self-gift in generative and faithful love. The celibate person renounces the realization of this capacity in marriage but embraces it in a universalizing love extended to all people. At the same time, the celibate commitment requires the development of particular habits and skills of living and relating in order to live the commitment with integrity. "Since the charism of celibacy, even when it is genuine and has proved itself, leaves man's affections and his instinctive impulses intact, candidates to the priesthood need an affective maturity which is prudent, able to renounce anything that is a threat to it, vigilant over both body and spirit, and capable of esteem and respect in interpersonal relationships between men and women" (*Pastores dabo vobis*, no. 44).

79.   Seminary formation in sexuality and celibacy must communicate to priesthood candidates and enable them to appropriate

- The physiological and psychological understanding of human sexuality
- The meaning of the virtue of chastity; this includes a formation in authentic ideals of sexual maturity and chastity, including virginity;[51] it also includes "a proper knowledge of the duties and dignity of Christian marriage, which represents the love which exists between Christ and the Church"[52]

---

51   See Sacred Congregation for Catholic Education, *A Guide to Formation in Priestly Celibacy* (1974), 46.
52   *Optatam totius*, no. 10.

- The requisite skills for living chastely: ascetical practice, prudent self-mastery, and paths of self-knowledge, such as a regular personal inventory and the examination of conscience
- The meaning of celibate chastity, especially the theological rationale that makes clear how it pertains to the logic of the ordained priesthood
- The means to live celibate chastity well, which include genuine friendships; priestly fraternity; a mentoring relationship; spiritual direction; priestly asceticism, which honestly reckons with the sacrifices that celibacy entails; and, especially, the sacrament of Penance
- The spiritual path that transforms the experience of loneliness into a holy solitude based on a "strong, lively, and personal love for Jesus Christ"[53]
- A cultural-critical attitude that discerns the positive and negative potentials of mass communications, various forms of entertainment, and technology, such as the Internet

80.   In general, human formation happens in a three-fold process of self-knowledge, self-acceptance, and self-gift—and all of this in faith.[54] As this process unfolds, the human person becomes more perfectly conformed to the perfect humanity of Jesus Christ, the Word made flesh.[55] The resources for fostering this process of human formation in a seminary context are many. They include

- *Instruction*: The rector and other faculty members offer the seminarians instruction in human formation through conferences, courses, and other educational means.
- *Personal reflection*: Seminarians are trained to live life reflectively and to examine, with regularity, their behavior, their motivations, their inclinations, and, in general, their appropriation of life experience, especially suffering.
- *Community life and feedback*: "A seminarian who freely chooses to enter a seminary must also freely accept and respect its terms."[56] The general demands and the rewards of life in community

↳ *correction*

---

53   *Pastores dabo vobis*, no. 44.
54   See United States Conference of Catholic Bishops, Committee on Priestly Formation, *Spiritual Formation in the Catholic Seminary* (1982).
55   See *A Guide to Formation in Priestly Celibacy*, 19.
56   *A Guide to Formation in Priestly Celibacy*, 74.

expand self-knowledge and self-control and cultivate generosity of spirit. The community's attachment to the Word of God and the sacramental life provides a reflective mirror that helps individuals know themselves and summons them to a fuller, more human, more spiritual life. A community's rule of life fosters discipline, self-mastery, and faithful perseverance in commitments.

- *Application to the tasks of seminary life*: Human formation develops through interaction with others in the course of the seminary program. This growth happens, for example, when seminarians learn to accept the authority of superiors, develop the habit of using freedom with discretion, learn to act on their own initiative and do so energetically, and learn to work harmoniously with confreres and laity.[57]

- *Formation advisors/mentors and directors*: Although the titles may differ, on every seminary faculty, certain members function as formators in the external forum. These formation advisors/mentors and directors should be priests. They observe seminarians and assist them to grow humanly by offering them feedback about their general demeanor, their relational capacities and styles, their maturity, their capacity to assume the role of a public person and leader in a community, and their appropriation of the human virtues that make them "men of communion." These same formators may, on occasion, teach the ways of human development and even offer some personal mentoring or, at times, coaching. More generally, they offer encouragement, support, and challenge along the formational path. These formators function exclusively in the external forum and are not to engage in matters that are reserved for the internal forum and the spiritual director.

- *Spiritual directors*: These priests, functioning in the internal forum, also play a role in the human formation of seminarians.[58] When they engage in the dialogue of spiritual direction with seminarians, they can be of great assistance in cultivating those virtues of self-reflection and self-discipline that are foundational for human development.

- *Psychological counseling*: On occasion, consultation with a psychologist or other licensed mental health professional can be a

For Mators

---

57   See *Optatam totius*, no. 11.
58   See Congregation for Institutes of Consecrated Life and Societies of Apostolic Life, *Letter to U.S. Bishops and Religious Superiors* (1990), 31.

useful instrument of human formation. Some patterns of behavior, for example, which became set in the candidate's early family history, may impede his relational abilities. Understanding one's psychological history and developing strategies to address elements of negative impact can be very helpful in human formation. This kind of counseling or consultation ought to be distinguished from extensive psychotherapy, which may be needed to address deeply entrenched personal issues that impede full functioning of the person. If such extensive and in-depth therapy is necessary, it ought to take place outside of the seminary context prior to the decision concerning admission; or, if the necessity for such therapy emerges after admission, then the student ought to withdraw from the program and pursue the therapy before being considered for re-admission to the seminary and resuming his advancement to orders.

81.   The norms and expectations of human formation for seminarians will, of course, vary according to the age of the person in formation as well as the particular stage of formation. One expects different levels of development in high school, college, pre-theology, and theology. It is advisable for each seminary to develop "markers of human formation" and identify them clearly for faculty and students. Resources for this can be found in *Pastores dabo vobis*, in the present document, and through a collaborative dialogue among seminary personnel across the nation.

82.   It is both possible and necessary to integrate human formation with the other three pillars of formation—the spiritual, the intellectual, and the pastoral. Human formation is linked to spiritual formation by the Incarnate Word and by the fact that grace builds on nature and perfects nature. Human formation is linked to intellectual formation by the cultivation of the human functions of perception, analysis, and judgment. It also contributes to intellectual formation by enabling seminarians to pursue theology as a response to the questions of the human condition. Human formation is finally linked to pastoral formation, which enables a priest to connect with and care for others with his human personality. Conversely, pastoral formation sharpens his human skills and empathic capacities.

NORMS FOR HUMAN FORMATION

Aim of the Human Formation Program

83.   Every seminary must have a program of human formation appropriate to the stage of the candidates' preparation, which seeks to prepare men to be bridges for, not obstacles to, the spread of the Gospel. The identity to be fostered in the candidate is that he becomes a man of communion, that is, someone who makes a gift of himself and is able to receive the gift of others. He needs integrity and self-possession in order to make such a gift. The capacity to be fostered is the affective ability to engage in pastoral leadership with Jesus as the model shepherd.[59]

84.   This program must have a clear focus on the ordained priesthood as a vocation that brings the candidates to full human and spiritual potential through love of God and service of others. Through conferences by the rector and by others and through other formation activities, as well as by the theology taught in the academic program, the seminary should make explicit the Church's doctrinal understanding of the ministerial priesthood on which its programs are based.

The Goals of Human Formation

85.   The qualities to be fostered in a human formation program are freedom, openness, honesty and flexibility, joy and inner peace, generosity and justice, personal maturity, interpersonal skills, common sense, aptitude for ministry, and growth "in moral sensibility and character."[60]

86.   Candidates should give evidence of having interiorized their seminary formation. Growth in self-awareness and sound personal identity are the hallmarks of a healthy personality that establishes a secure basis for the spiritual life. Such growth may be demonstrated by sound prudential judgment; sense of responsibility and personal initiative; a capacity for courageous and decisive leadership; an ability to establish and maintain wholesome friendships; and an ability to work in a collaborative, profes-

---

59   See the Association of Theological Schools (ATS), Pittsburgh, *Standard A*, A 3.1.3. Cf. CCEO, c. 346§2, 8°: "Let them also esteem and cultivate those virtues that are most valued by people and commend the minister of Christ, among which are sincerity, a keen concern for justice, a spirit of poverty, fidelity to one's promises, good manners, modesty in conversation joined with charity."
60   ATS *Standard A*, A 4.1.1.

sional manner with women and men, foregoing self-interests in favor of cooperative effort for the common good.

The Candidate for Human Formation

87.   Candidates bear the primary responsibility for their human formation. The role of the seminary is to assist them in achieving the aims of the *Program of Priestly Formation*.

88.   The candidate's human formation in the seminary is very much affected by the character formation he has received in his family, cultural background, and society. Just as the seminary recognizes that the positive qualities of a seminarian's prior formation can both indicate a vocation and provide a solid foundation for further growth, it should also address possible deficiencies in the candidate's earlier formation and find means to address them.

89.   Human formation programs in the seminary should begin with the assumption that the candidates have the potential to move from self-preoccupation to an openness to transcendent values and a concern for the welfare of others; a history of sound and rewarding peer relationships; an ability to be honest with themselves and with others; and an ability to trust the Church and the agents of formation. Formation programs will not be very effective for those who manifest extreme inflexibility, narcissism, antisocial behavior or any other serious pathology, a lack of sexual integration, a deep and unresolved anger (especially against authority), a deep attachment to a materialist lifestyle, or compulsive behaviors or addictions.

Preparation for Celibacy

90.   Preparation for celibacy is one of the primary aims of the human formation program of any seminary. The seminary must have a coordinated and multifaceted program of instruction, prayerful discernment, dialogue, and encouragement that will aid seminarians to understand the nature and purpose of celibate chastity and to embrace it wholeheartedly in their lives. Sexuality finds its authentic meaning in relation to mature love. Seminarians should understand and manifest a mature love as preparation for a celibate life. In doing so, the insights of modern psychology can be a considerable aid. The goal of psychosexual, social, and spiritual

development should be to form seminarians into chaste, celibate men who are loving pastors of the people they serve.[61]

91.   The rector should hold periodic conferences on this topic, at least on a yearly basis, in which basic attitudinal and behavioral expectations about the practice of celibacy for priests and candidates for the priesthood are detailed. He should clearly delineate the kinds of attitudes and behaviors that are acceptable and praiseworthy and the kinds that are not. He should address the responsibilities, both now and later, of individual seminarians, for themselves and for the common reputation of the community and the priesthood. Clear, concrete terms must be used about the actual meaning of the celibate commitment in the seminary community, and later in priestly ministry, if presentations about the value of celibacy are to be persuasive or taken seriously.

92.   Human formation for celibacy should aim toward an affective maturity, which is the ability to live a true and responsible love. Signs of affective maturity in the candidate are prudence, vigilance over body and spirit, compassion and care for others, ability to express and acknowledge emotions, and a capacity to esteem and respect interpersonal relationships between men and women. Therefore, true friendship is an education in affective maturity.

93.   To live fully an effective life of celibate chastity requires (a) a knowledge of one's sexuality and sexual desires; (b) an acceptance and valuing of one's sexuality as a good to be directed to God's service; (c) a lifelong commitment to growth, which means continuously integrating one's sexuality into a life and ministry shaped and expressed by celibate chastity. Certain habits or skills are necessary instruments on the path to effective and healthy celibate chastity, and these are to be encouraged in seminary programs. Among these habits and skills are appropriate self- disclosure, a cultivated capacity for self-reflection, an ability to enter into peaceful solitude, ascetical practices that foster vigilance and self mastery over one's impulses and drives, and a habit of modesty. An especially important practice is holding all persons in the mystery of God, whether they are encountered in the course of formal ministry or ordinary life. This practice means viewing all persons in God, interceding for them before God, and claiming responsibility to direct them to God.

---

61   See *Pastores dabo vobis*, no. 44.

94.   A seminary human formation program should inculcate additional skills for celibate living as care for others, a deepening of the capacity to give and receive love, an ability to practice appropriate self-disclosure, an ability to develop and maintain healthy and inclusive peer friendships, and an ability to set appropriate boundaries by choosing not to act on romantic feelings and by developing self-discipline in the face of temptation. A candidate must be prepared to accept wholeheartedly the Church's teaching on sexuality in its entirety, be determined to master all sexual temptations, be prepared to meet the challenge of living chastely in all friendships, and, finally, be resolved to fashion his sexual desires and passions in such a way that he is able to live a healthy, celibate lifestyle that expresses self-gift in faithful and life-giving love: being attentive to others, helping them reach their potential, not giving up, and investing all one's energies in the service of the Kingdom of God.

95.   The seminary must have written guidelines for admission, evaluation, and community life that spell out its expectations regarding those attitudes, behaviors, and levels of psychosexual maturity that indicate a right mentality, proper motivation, and a commitment to celibate chastity. These guidelines should also specify unacceptable attitudes and behaviors that militate against such a commitment.

96.   Any credible evidence in the candidate of a sexual attraction to children necessitates an immediate dismissal from the seminary.

Preparation for a Simplicity of Life

97.   Human formation should cultivate a spirit of generosity, encouraging the seminarian to become a man for others and to curb expectations of entitlement. Manifestations of undue materialism and consumerism in the seminarian's behavior should be confronted and corrected.

98.   The formation program should articulate the distinctive qualities of simplicity of life appropriate for one preparing for priestly leadership. Simplicity of life is particularly important in our own age when human needs and desires are so consciously manipulated and exploited. A consumer society often reduces people to things, which are used and then discarded, plunging society more deeply into a world of objects, which ironically seem to possess us. In a consumer society, a right attitude toward the world and earthly goods is easily lost. That is why a seminarian has to be helped to cultivate personal self-discipline and asceticism. It is an important pastoral

obligation of all priests who accompany people through the journey of life to acquire a sound and balanced perspective about earthly goods and possessions so that they can impart right attitudes to others.

99.   The seminary should foster simplicity of life. Such an attitude is not disparaging of the world but sees it in light of freedom and service. Priests are able to understand correctly "that the Church's mission is carried out in the midst of the world and that created goods are absolutely necessary for man's personal progress."[62] They can also better appreciate that when the passion for acquisition and possession is curbed, the human capacity for appreciation and enjoyment of the world often is enhanced.

Preparation for Obedience

100.   The seminary should articulate appropriate behaviors which manifest a healthy understanding of obedience. The exercise of authority and the response of obedience are works of grace, goodwill, and human effort that play a part in the life of every priest. Seminarians should appreciate and integrate the necessary role that authority and organization play in achieving and maintaining any community's goals and purposes, as well as recognize the spiritual dimension of authority and obedience in the Catholic Church. Certainly, the pursuit of truth is the aim of all Christians. In that process, seminarians must manifest in heart and mind adherence to the Word of God and the Magisterium.[63]

101.   Seminaries should expect of seminarians a spirit of joyful trust, open dialogue, and generous cooperation with those in authority. As seminarians advance in their training they should be given more opportunity to exercise responsibility and freedom. At the same time, they should understand that accountability is always part of the exercise of freedom.

102.   Seminaries should articulate that priestly obedience begins with humble and willing cooperation in seminary life, docility to direction, and wholehearted compliance with the seminary's policies and programs. This will prepare seminarians to cooperate with their bishop[64] or superior, espe-

---

62   *Presbyterorum ordinis*, no. 17.
63   See CIC, cc. 748§1 and 750-754; CCEO, cc. 10, 598-600, 1436.
64   See *Presbyterorum ordinis*, no. 7: "Priests for their part . . . should [respect in their bishop] the authority of Christ the supreme Pastor. They should therefore be attached to their bishop with sincere charity and obedience."

cially in the very practical matter of undertaking and faithfully fulfilling whatever sacred duty is given to them.[65]

Resources for Human Formation

103.   The rector of the seminary has the responsibility to delineate attitudinal and behavioral expectations regarding all aspects of human formation, especially those which are appropriate to a life of celibacy, a life of simplicity, and a life of obedience.

104.   Seminary faculty should provide the guidance and direction necessary to help seminarians meet the challenge of emotional and psychosexual growth. In the area of emotional and personal development the best guidance the seminary faculty can give is the wholesome witness of their own lives. The priest members of the faculty form an important subgroup within the seminary community. Seminarians need the example of outstanding priests who model a wholesome way of life in the challenging circumstances of contemporary society. Regularly coming together for prayer, recreation, and theological reflection encourages growth in priestly fraternity and enables priests to act more effectively as authentic role models. The entire seminary staff, composed of priests, religious, and laity, constitutes another significant group, who can model collegiality for the seminarians. Ways to foster the unity of this larger circle should also be developed.

105.   The rector or his delegate should make provision for psychological and counseling services. He therefore ensures that those employed as counselors for seminarians are professionally licensed/certified and well versed in and supportive of the Church's expectations of candidates for the priesthood, especially concerning celibacy, and that they will not encourage behaviors contrary to church teachings. These services are made available to seminarians for their personal and emotional development as candidates for the priesthood. The counseling that is given should be consistent with the policy and practice of the total seminary program. Counseling is often a helpful tool in the candidate's human formation. Its role, however, should not be overestimated. While psychology and the human sciences can be resources for human formation, they are not

---

65   See Second Vatican Council, *Christus Dominus* (*Decree Concerning the Pastoral Office of Bishops in the Church*) (1965), no. 28.

the same as human formation. Seminaries should draw up guidelines for psychologists describing objectively those traits and attitudes that indicate satisfactory progress toward the priesthood and those that indicate a lack of the requisite qualities needed for growth in human formation. The basis for such guidelines are the qualities articulated in this document. Seminarians in need of long-term therapy should avail themselves of such assistance before entering the seminary, or should leave the program until the therapy has been completed. If such a departure be indicated, there should be no expectation of automatic readmission. A candidate should not be considered for advancement to Holy Orders if he is engaged in long-term psychological therapy. Issues being addressed in counseling should be satisfactorily settled prior to the call to Holy Orders. Clear and prudent guidelines are necessary for fostering the personal, emotional, and psychosexual development of seminarians in the context of a wholesome community.

II. SPIRITUAL FORMATION

106.   Human formation leads to and finds its completion in spiritual formation. Human formation continues in conjunction with and in coordination with the spiritual, intellectual, and pastoral dimensions of formation. It steadily points to the center, which is spiritual formation. "For every priest his spiritual formation is the core which unifies and gives life to his *being* a priest and his *acting as* a priest" (Pastores dabo vobis, no. 45).

107.   The basic principle of spiritual formation is contained in *Pastores dabo vobis*, no. 45, and is a synthesis of the teachings in *Optatam totius*: to live in intimate and unceasing union with God the Father through his Son, Jesus Christ, in the Holy Spirit. This is the foundational call to discipleship and conversion of heart. Those who aspire to be sent on mission, as the apostles were, must first acquire the listening and learning heart of disciples. Jesus invited these apostles to come to him before he sent them out to others. St. Augustine alluded to this double identity and commitment as disciple and apostle, when he said to his people, "With you I am a Christian, for you I am a bishop."[66]

108.   To live in intimate and unceasing union with God the Father through his Son Jesus Christ in the Holy Spirit is far more than a personal

---

66   *Sermo*, 46, 1-2.

or individual relationship with the Lord; it is also a communion with the Church, which is his body. The spirituality that belongs to those who are priests or preparing for priesthood is at one and the same time Trinitarian, Christological, pneumatological, and ecclesial. It is a spirituality of communion rooted in the mystery of the Triune God and lived out in practical ways in the mystery of ecclesial communion.

109.   The spirituality cultivated in the seminary is specifically priestly. Through the Sacraments of Initiation, seminarians already share in the Paschal Mystery of Jesus Christ with other members of the Church. They also aspire to become priests who are configured to Christ, Head and Shepherd of the Church, our great high Priest. Therefore, their spirituality draws them into the priestly, self-sacrificial path of Jesus. He is the one whose service finds its high point in giving his life as a ransom for the many.[67] He is the Good Shepherd who lays down his life for his sheep "so that they might have life and have it more abundantly."[68] He is the bridegroom who loves his bride, the Church, "and handed himself over for her."[69]

110.   Given these basic dimensions of priestly spirituality that are foundational to the program of spiritual formation in the seminary, the seminary should identify those characteristics and practices that foster its growth. It is a formation that includes

- *Holy Eucharist*: Spiritual formation is first and foremost a participation in public worship of the Church that is itself a participation in the heavenly liturgy offered by Christ, our great high priest. "We have such a high priest, who has taken his seat at the right hand of the throne of the Majesty in heaven."[70] The Eucharistic sacrifice is both spiritual sustenance, the Bread of Life, and the transformation of our lives by the power of the self-giving and redeeming love of Jesus Christ, crucified and risen. It is the source of pastoral charity, the love that animates and directs those who walk in the footsteps of the Good Shepherd, who gives his life for his sheep so that they may live. As source and summit

---

67   See Mk 10:45.
68   Jn 10:10; see Jn 10:17-18.
69   Eph 5:25; see Eph 5:26-27.
70   Heb 8:1.

of the Christian life, the daily celebration of the Eucharist is the "essential moment of the day."[71]

- *Sacrament of Penance*: The Sacrament of Penance fosters the mature recognition of sin, continuous conversion of heart, growth in the virtues, and conformity to the mind of Christ. It is a school of compassion that teaches penitents how to live out God's compassionate mercy in the world. The frequent celebration of the Sacrament of Penance is aided by the practice of a daily examination of conscience (CIC, 276§2, 5°).

- *Liturgy of the Hours*: Through the Liturgy of the Hours, seminarians learn to pray with the Church and for the Church. They unite themselves with the Body of Christ in unceasing praise and petition. This prayer prepares them for their lifelong ministry as priests who pray on behalf of the whole Church. It also cultivates a mind and heart attuned to the whole Body of Christ, its needs, its sufferings, its graces, and its hopes.[72]

- *Spiritual direction*: A regular meeting (at least once a month) with an approved spiritual director is an essential part of spiritual direction, especially in arriving at the interiorization and integration needed for growth in sanctity, virtue, and readiness for Holy Orders.

- *Bible*: Receiving the Word of God proclaimed and preached in the Church or the quiet and personal assimilation of that holy Word in *lectio divina* enables those in formation to hear God's communication to them as a transforming challenge and hope. To take on more fully the mind of Christ and to be steadily transformed by the Word of God, the seminarian ought to develop the habit of daily reflection on the Sacred Scriptures, by daily meditation on the lectionary readings and/or other reflective reading of the Scriptures.[73]

- *Retreats and days of recollection*: Regular periods of more intensive prayer will be part of the seminary year.

- *Personal meditation*: The habit of daily prayer and meditation enables seminarians to acquire a personalized sense of how God's salvation has taken hold of their lives and how they might respond to that great grace. This prayer happens in a context of silence

---

71 *Pastores dabo vobis*, no. 46; see *Ecclesia de Eucharistia*.
72 See *Pastores dabo vobis*, no. 48.
73 See *Pastores dabo vobis*, no. 47.

and solitude in which they learn to be attuned to God's movements in their lives. It grows and develops into a "contemplative attitude" that learns to find God in all things. It matures in such a way that it allows for a balanced and unified rhythm of life in action and contemplation, work and prayer, while providing the future priest with the strength, meaning, and focus he will need in his life.

- *Devotions*: Devotional prayer, especially centered on Eucharistic Adoration, the Blessed Virgin Mary—in particular, the rosary—and the saints, assists seminarians in assimilating the mystery of Christ and hearing the invitation to live that mystery in the particular circumstances of their own life. Devotional prayer helps to sustain affective communion with the Lord and his Church. It also helps them to connect with the rich cultural diversity of devotional life in the United States and to appreciate devotional practices of other cultures.

- *Apostolic dimensions*: Spiritual formation also involves seeking Christ in people.[74] Especially in a seminary context, seminarians are to learn how prayer is to be lived out in service of others, particularly the poor, the sick, sinners, unbelievers, and the stranger, but extended to all in the outreach of charity and mercy, and in the quest for justice. Prayer is apostolic also in the sense that seminarians learn to pray for the needs of those they serve in order to teach others how to pray. Whatever growth and formation in prayer takes place, it is not simply meant for the personal enhancement of the seminarian but as a gift to be given in the course of his priestly mission and ministry for the benefit of the Church—for he is a servant of this body.

- *Asceticism and Penance*: Spiritual formation initiates seminarians to a path of voluntary renunciation and self-denial that makes them more available to the will of God and more available to their people. Asceticism and the practice of penance is a path of learning to embrace the cross and, in an apostolic context, a way of rendering priests unafraid to bear their "share of hardship for the gospel with the strength that comes from God" (2 Tm 1:8).

- *Obedience*: The obedience of those in spiritual formation for priesthood must be characterized by the willingness to hear God

---

74   See *Pastores dabo vobis*, no. 49.

who speaks through his Word and through his Church and to answer his call with generosity. It is also a surrender of one's own will for the sake of the larger mission. In this regard, the candidate for priesthood must develop a growing and deepening solidarity with the Church established by Christ, a solidarity with Church teaching so as to be able to present that teaching with conviction—having appropriated it as true—and a solidarity with ecclesial leadership to strengthen and sustain Church unity.

- *Celibacy*: Spiritual formation in celibacy cultivates the evangelical motivations for embracing this commitment and way of life: the undivided love of the Lord, the spousal love for the Church, apostolic availability, and the witness to God's promises and kingdom.[75]

- *Simplicity of life*: Spiritual formation encourages a simple approach to the material goods of this world. Freed from excessive concern about possessions, priests and seminarians and, particularly, religious are able to serve in an unencumbered way. To live with evangelical simplicity is to exercise responsible stewardship over God's creation by using material goods in a way that is both responsive to the call of the Gospel and ecologically responsible. The witness of a genuine simplicity of life is especially important in the context of American affluence. Spiritual directors and mentors/advisors must be sensitive to seminarians' stewardship of their own, the seminary's, and the Church's material resources. Spiritual formation for simplicity of life and stewardship flows directly from striving to have the mind of Christ Jesus, "who, though he was in the form of God, / did not regard equality with God something to be grasped. / Rather, he emptied himself . . ." (Phil 2:6-7a). This is the Lord Jesus who, again according to St. Paul, "for your sake . . . became poor although he was rich, so that by his poverty you might become rich" (2 Cor 8:9).

- *Reconciliation*: Spiritual formation fosters a reconciling spirit in those who aspire to be priests in the spirit of Jesus, who prayed that "all might be one." A peacemaking and nonviolent way of life marks out those who have been entrusted with the ministry of reconciliation.[76] The power that is entrusted to God's ministers, a power that takes many forms, must always be used for the

leads to MERCY

---

75   See *Pastores dabo vobis*, no. 50.
76   See 2 Cor 5:18.

good, peaceably, and in a way that expresses the trust invested in God's priests.

- *Solidarity*: The post-synodal exhortation *Ecclesia in America* identified the critical importance of the path of solidarity for the Church in the American hemisphere. "'Solidarity is thus the fruit of the communion which is grounded in the mystery of the triune God, and in the Son of God who took flesh and died for all. It is expressed in Christian love which seeks the good of others, especially of those most in need.' . . . For the particular Churches of the American continent, this is the source of a commitment to reciprocal solidarity and the sharing of the spiritual gifts and material goods with which God has blessed them, fostering in individuals a readiness to work where they are needed."[77] This means that seminarians are to have a spiritual formation grounded in Trinitarian communion that leads them to solidarity with others, especially those most in need, a commitment to justice and peace, a reciprocal exchange of spiritual and material gifts, and an authentic missionary spirit expressed in a willingness to serve where needed.

- *Solitude*: Spiritual formation must not neglect the art of "being alone with God," moving the candidate from being alone or lonely to entering a holy solitude in communion with God.

- *Ongoing spiritual formation*: The final goal of spiritual formation in the seminary is to establish attitudes, habits, and practices in the spiritual life that will continue after ordination. Spiritual formation in the seminary is meant to set the foundation for a lifetime of priestly ministry and spirituality.

111. The development of sound and lasting habits and attitudes in the spiritual life is a challenging process. Intensive spiritual formation experiences, for example, a Spirituality Year Program, a thirty-day retreat, a summer program, etc., are valuable means for facilitating this process and should be considered for possible inclusion and integration into the seminary program.

112. Spiritual formation needs to be integrated with the other three pillars of formation—the human, the intellectual, and the pastoral. From

---

77   *Ecclesia in America*, no. 52.

human formation, spiritual formation assumes that the candidate has a basic relational capacity. In other words, the seminarian is able to enter into significant, even deep, relationships with other persons and with God. He is to be a "man of communion."

113. Intellectual formation contributes to spiritual formation. The study of the traditions of faith and the experiences of faith among the saints and the people of God serves to deepen one's own spiritual journey.

114. Pastoral formation is intimately linked with spiritual formation. In the process of spiritual formation, candidates are called to a greater and wider-ranging love of God and neighbor. When they respond positively to this invitation and grow in that love, they find the basis for pastoral and ministerial outreach that culminates in pastoral charity.

115. Since spiritual formation is the core that unifies the life of a priest, it stands at the heart of seminary life and is the center around which all other aspects are integrated. Human, intellectual, and pastoral formation are indispensable in developing the seminarian's relationship and communion with God and his ability to communicate God's truth and love to others in the likeness of Jesus Christ, the Good Shepherd and eternal High Priest.

NORMS FOR SPIRITUAL FORMATION

Prayer

116. The celebration of the Eucharist takes place daily and every member of the community ordinarily participates.[78] This includes a regularly scheduled Saturday morning Mass and Sunday community Mass. All priests who are not bound to celebrate individually for the pastoral benefit of the faithful should concelebrate at the community Mass insofar as possible.[79] Priest-faculty members concelebrate when they are present for Mass.

---

78 See CIC, c. 246§1; CCEO, c. 346§2, 2°.
79 See *General Instruction of the Roman Missal* (Washington, DC: United States Conference of Catholic Bishops, 2003), no. 114.

117.   The seminary community must schedule the Liturgy of the Hours, especially Morning and Evening Prayer, on a daily basis.[80]

118.   The careful preparation and execution of liturgical celebrations should be supervised by the seminary director of liturgy. Because the liturgical life of the seminary shapes the sensitivities and attitudes of seminarians for future ministry, an authentic sense of the holy mysteries should be carefully preserved in all liturgical celebrations along with a care for their beauty and dignity (see *Ecclesia de Eucharistia*, no. 5). The laws and prescriptions of approved liturgical books are normative. Priest faculty should be particularly observant of the liturgical rubrics and avoid the insertion of any personal liturgical adaptations, unless they are authorized by the liturgical books.[81] The seminary liturgy should also promote in seminarians a respect for legitimate, rubrically approved liturgical expressions of cultural diversity as well as the Church's ancient liturgical patrimony.[82] Priest-faculty should always be aware that they have a particular and serious responsibility to model for seminarians the proper way to preside at the sacraments, especially the Eucharist. All other teachers of liturgy as well as directors of music at the seminary are to be supportive of this norm.

119.   Instruction should be given concerning the meaning and proper celebration of the Eucharist and the Liturgy of the Hours and their benefits for spiritual growth in the seminary and for the communities that seminarians later will serve. Seminarians must be instructed to incorporate progressively all of the hours of the Liturgy of the Hours, beginning with Morning Prayer and Evening Prayer, and then the Office of Readings, and, finally, the Daytime Hour and Night Prayer. This entire cycle should be a regular practice of each seminarian at least a year prior to his diaconate ordination.

120.   Catechesis must be given concerning the Sacrament of Penance and its importance for priestly ministry and life. Communal celebrations of the Sacrament of Penance should be scheduled regularly, especially during Advent and Lent. The seminary must schedule frequent opportunities at various times during the week and encourage the individual celebration of the Sacrament of Penance. The seminary should ensure that other

---

80   See CIC, c. 246§2; CCEO, c. 346§2, 3°.
81   See *Ecclesia de Eucharistia*, no. 52.
82   See *Ecclesia de Eucharistia*, no. 49-51; *General Instruction of the Roman Missal*, no. 41.

confessors for the Sacrament of Penance are available on a regular basis.[83] A priest-faculty member who has sole responsibility for external formation is not to hear seminarians' confessions, nor may he comment on a seminarian-penitent's advancement.[84] Each seminarian is encouraged to have a regular confessor, who ideally is also his spiritual director, with whom he can be completely honest, fully manifesting his conscience, and from whom he can receive ongoing guidance. This is not meant to limit the penitent's liberty, since he is always free to approach other confessors, whether in the seminary or outside it.[85]

121.   The seminary program and spiritual direction should teach seminarians to value solitude and personal prayer as a necessary part of priestly spirituality. Occasions for silence and properly directed solitude should be provided during retreats and days of recollection.[86] An atmosphere of quiet should be provided within the seminary community on a daily basis to ensure an environment conducive for prayer.

122.   Conferences, days of recollection, workshops, and retreats should be well organized and sponsored by the seminary and form a whole and coherent program of spiritual formation. An annual retreat of at least five days must be a part of the theologate program.[87]

123.   Guidance and instruction in methods of meditation, contemplation, *lectio divina*, and daily examen must be provided.

124.   Devotion to the Blessed Sacrament must be encouraged. Scheduled hours of eucharistic exposition are particularly desirable to provide for special opportunities for the adoration of the Blessed Sacrament in the seminary. It is also desirable that seminarians develop a habit of personal visits to the Blessed Sacrament in the tabernacle.

125.   Devotion to the Blessed Virgin Mary, the Mother of God, and to the saints must be encouraged.[88] Opportunities for devotional prayer should be made available and encouraged. The rosary, "a compendium

---

83   See CIC, cc. 240§1, 246§4; CCEO, cc. 339§2, 346§2.
84   See CIC, c. 240§2; CCEO, c. 339§3.
85   See CIC, c. 240§1; CCEO, c. 339§2.
86   See CIC, c. 246§5; CCEO, c. 346§2, 6°.
87   See CIC, c. 246§5. CCEO, c. 346§2, 6°.
88   See CIC, c. 246§3; CCEO, c. 346§2, 5°.

of the Gospel,"[89] is especially recommended as a means of contemplating Christ "in the school of Mary."[90]

126. The seminary should sponsor, on appropriate occasions, ecumenical events, including prayer services, with other Christians. Consideration should also be given to interaction with those of other religions.

Spiritual Direction

127. Seminarians should meet regularly, no less than once a month, with a priest spiritual director.[91] Spiritual directors must be chosen from a list prepared by the director of spiritual formation. They should have proper training and adequate credentials for the work. These priests must be approved by the rector and appointed by the diocesan bishop or religious ordinary.[92] In the case of religious seminarians, the formation director or religious superior offers guidance on an appropriate spiritual director for the seminarians under his care.

128. Seminarians should confide their personal history, personal relationships, prayer experiences, the cultivation of virtues, their temptations, and other significant topics to their spiritual director. If, for serious reason, there is a change of director, the new director ought to give attention to continuity in the seminarian's spiritual development.

129. The spiritual director should foster an integration of spiritual formation, human formation, and character development consistent with priestly formation. The spiritual director assists the seminarian in acquiring the skills of spiritual discernment and plays a key role in helping the seminarian discern whether he is called to priesthood or to another vocation in the Church.

130. Those priests who do spiritual direction for seminarians must understand and support the full formation program. They also need to be integrated into the priestly community of the seminary. The spiritual

---

89   Pius XII, "Letter to the Archbishop of Manila," *Philippinas insulas* (AAS 38 [1946] 419). See Paul VI, *Marialis cultus* (*For the Right Ordering and Development of Devotion to the Blessed Virgin Mary*) (1974), no. 42; John Paul II, *Rosarium Virginis Mariae* (*On the Most Holy Rosary*) (2002), no. 1.
90   *Rosarium Virginis Mariae*, no. 1 (Washington, DC: United States Conference of Catholic Bishops, 2002).
91   See CIC, c. 246§4; CCEO, c. 346§2, 4°.
92   See CIC, c. 239§2; CCEO, c. 339§1.

directors are thus aware that they are part of the whole seminary program and community.

131.   Care should be taken to ensure that issues of human formation that properly belong to the external forum are not limited to the spiritual direction relationship for their resolution.

132.   Because spiritual direction in a seminary context differs from spiritual direction more generally experienced in the Church, the seminary must explain to seminarians the purpose and process of spiritual direction in the seminary. This should include, for example: an understanding that spiritual direction is not an optional possibility but a seminary requirement; a recognition that seminary spiritual direction is concerned not only with the personal spiritual growth of seminarians but also with their preparation for service in the Church as priests; a knowledge that the spiritual direction process must take into account the limited time of the program and preparation for ordination and that, therefore, one ought to have passed certain thresholds of spiritual development and commitment at different points in the seminary program (in contrast to the open-ended nature of non-seminary spiritual direction); and an acceptance that a lack of readiness for spiritual direction itself ought to prompt a student to question his continuance in the seminary at this time and seriously to consider withdrawing from the program until he is ready.

133.   Meetings with spiritual directors should be of sufficient frequency and duration to allow adequate opportunity to assist the seminarian in ongoing vocational discernment, proximate preparation for the reception of ministries and orders, and formation for celibacy.

134.   Disclosures that a seminarian makes in the course of spiritual direction belong to the internal forum. Consequently, the spiritual director is held to the strictest confidentiality concerning information received in spiritual direction. He may neither reveal it nor use it.[93] The only possible exception to this standard of confidentiality would be the case of grave, immediate, or mortal danger involving the directee or another person. If what is revealed in spiritual direction coincides with the celebration of the Sacrament of Penance (in other words, what is revealed is revealed *ad ordinem absolutionis*), that is, the exchange not only takes place in the internal

---

93   See CIC, c. 240§2; CCEO, c. 339§3.

forum but also the sacramental forum, then the absolute strictures of the seal of confession hold, and no information may be revealed or used.

135. Although the rector may never ask a spiritual director about the content of a seminarian's conversation, he can expect a spiritual director to confirm that a seminarian sees him at least monthly. The spiritual director should notify the rector if the director decides to discontinue spiritual direction with any student or if the student discontinues direction with him.

III. INTELLECTUAL FORMATION

136. There is a reciprocal relationship between spiritual and intellectual formation. The intellectual life nourishes the spiritual life, but the spiritual also opens vistas of understanding, in accordance with the classical adage *credo ut intelligam* ('I believe in order to know'). Intellectual formation is integral to what it means to be human. "Intellectual formation . . . is a fundamental demand of man's intelligence by which he 'participates in the light of God's mind' and seeks to acquire a wisdom which in turn opens to and is directed towards knowing and adhering to God" (*Pastores dabo vobis*, no. 51, citing *Gaudium et spes*, no. 15).

137. The basic principle of intellectual formation for priesthood candidates is noted in *Pastores dabo vobis*, no. 51: "For the salvation of their brothers and sisters, they should seek an ever deeper knowledge of the divine mysteries." Disciples are learners. The first task of intellectual formation is to acquire a personal knowledge of the Lord Jesus Christ, who is the fullness and completion of God's revelation and the one Teacher. This saving knowledge is acquired not only once, but it is continuously appropriated and deepened, so that it becomes more and more part of us. Seminary intellectual formation assumes and prolongs the catechesis and mystagogia that is to be part of every Christian's journey of faith. At the same time, this knowledge is not simply for personal possession but is destined to be shared in the community of faith. And that is why it is "for the salvation of their brothers and sisters." Intellectual formation has an apostolic and missionary purpose and finality.

138. In the seminary program, intellectual formation culminates in a deepened understanding of the mysteries of faith that is pastorally oriented toward effective priestly ministry, especially preaching. This understanding,

however, requires previous intellectual formation and academic integrity as foundational. The overall goal of every stage of seminary formation is to prepare a candidate who is widely knowledgeable about the human condition, deeply engaged in a process of understanding divine revelation, and adequately skilled in communicating his knowledge to as many people as possible. Moreover, continuing education after ordination is a necessity for effective ministry.

139.   The intellectual formation of the candidate must be directed to the ecclesial dimensions of priestly formation, namely, the teaching office (*munus docendi*) of the priesthood. The doctrinal, educational, catechetical, and apologetical aspects of a candidate's training are to prepare the seminarian to be a faithful, loyal, and authentic teacher of the Gospel. As a man of the Church, the priest preaches and teaches in fidelity to the magisterium, particularly the Holy Father and the diocesan bishop. The intellectual formation program must emphasize the intrinsic relationship between the knowledge gained in theological preparation and the ecclesial dimensions of priestly service, since the education of a priest is never seen in isolation from the Tradition of the Church.

> for the 21st century

THE CONTEXT OF INTELLECTUAL FORMATION

140.   The context of intellectual formation in the United States at the beginning of the twenty-first century is important to note, because it highlights the specific challenges that both seminaries and seminarians face in the process of intellectual formation. Among the elements of context are the following:

- Many candidates approach the seminary with significant educational background. They are, however, often narrowly educated, that is, they may have great expertise in a particular area and have a high level of technical training, but lack a wide background. Often lacking is education in the humanities, which would enable them to study theology effectively and make pastoral connections with the lives of the people whom they will serve.
- Older candidates approach the seminary with considerable life experience, but they may have lost contact with formal patterns of study in school. Their age may seem to warrant that they be moved through the seminarian program quickly, or that they be

given a program that has been reduced in expectations. This lat-
ter trend, however, is to be resisted.

- International candidates may arrive at the seminary with a
limited knowledge of the English language as well as a limited
understanding of United States culture. These limitations present significant challenges for teaching and learning. Unless there
is sufficient familiarity with language and culture, the study of
theology will be severely impeded.

- Candidates coming from a United States cultural context, even
though they may be young and have had exposure to the liberal arts in college, may bring with them the limitations of the
culture's understanding of the human person as well as the limitations of a philosophical milieu that is suspicious of enduring,
absolute moral values and objective truths. Unless these candidates are grounded in an adequate philosophical and theological
anthropology, they will struggle to make sense of their theological
studies and its application in pastoral practice.

- Candidates apply to seminary programs with backgrounds of varied
religious experiences and varied levels of catechetical formation.

STAGES IN PREPARATION FOR THEOLOGY

141.   There are four possible preparatory stages of seminary formation prior to the study of theology and immediate preparation for priestly
ordination and ministry. They include high school seminary, college seminary, cultural preparation programs, and pre-theology. These preparatory
phases are explained in the following paragraphs.

High School Seminary

142.   In the high school seminary, students acquire the basic skills
and knowledge that enable them to pursue higher education. Catechesis
should occupy a central position in the program of a high school seminary. This should include a solid foundation in spirituality and Catholic
moral values.

143.   A good high school education is a value in itself and an important step in the development of a priestly vocation. The primary intellectual goal of a high-school-level seminary program should be a well-
rounded secondary education as a preparation for college. Such formation

must present the best available academic program, taking into consideration the needs of the student and the multicultural character of today's Church. It should combine creativity, sound pedagogy, and a concern for academic standards.

144.   A good high school education must meet the educational requirements of local and state accreditation agencies. In addition, a high school seminary program should strive for excellence and take the necessary steps for students to achieve it. Good teachers, well-prepared courses, and a coherent and well-planned curriculum, which provides remedial courses when necessary, are all elements that compose a good high school education.

145.   The academic program of a high school seminary should be sensitive to the multicultural character of its student body.

College Seminary

146.   In the college seminary, students follow a double course of intellectual formation. They first pursue the liberal arts, through which they acquire a sense of the great human questions contained in the arts and sciences. They synthesize and organize their study of the liberal arts through the study of philosophy, which also serves as a preparation for the study of theology. This two-fold college program also initiates students to the study of theology that will, of course, be pursued in greater depth in the theologate. A good college seminary program promotes excellence and takes necessary steps for students to achieve it.

Liberal Arts

147.   A sound liberal arts education for candidates preparing for the priesthood provides multiple benefits. The study of the natural world and of humanity in all its historical and cultural diversity represents a significant value in its own right. Such an education encourages intellectual curiosity, promotes critical thought, and fosters disciplined habits of study. A liberal arts education also teaches students to communicate with others in a clear and effective way.

148.   A liberal arts education gives students an introduction into the wider range of human learning. Studies in mathematics and natural science, in the social and behavioral sciences, in history, literature,

foreign languages—both ancient (Latin and Greek) and modern—communication skills, and the fine arts define the content of a liberal arts curriculum.

149.   A liberal education also has a special value as a preparation for the study of theology. The liberal arts have traditionally provided college-level candidates with an understanding of the cultural roots of their faith. By understanding the human sciences, they can comprehend better the world in which God acts. By grasping how faith and culture have interacted in the past, they gain some insight into the working of God's plan in larger historical events.

150.   The curriculum should also strive to take into consideration contemporary issues of the day in intellectual, cultural, social, economic, and political life as they pertain to moral and religious topics. Such an approach stimulates students to deeper study by building on current knowledge and interests. The authentic teaching of the Church on such issues should be clearly and cogently presented. The curriculum should introduce students to the basic teachings of the faith as well as to the richness and diversity of the Catholic intellectual tradition.

151.   A liberal arts education normally involves a field of concentrated study. Philosophy has historically been considered the most appropriate area of concentration for college seminarians. Every college seminary should offer philosophy as the preferred major field of study. Other liberal arts may be appropriate fields of concentration for some students. The choice of another major should be evaluated on an individual basis.

Philosophy

152.   "The study of philosophy is fundamental and indispensable to the structure of theological studies and to the formation of candidates for the priesthood. It is not by chance that the curriculum of theological studies is preceded by a time of special study of philosophy."[94] In priestly formation, at least two full years should be dedicated to the philosophical

---

94   John Paul II, *Fides et ratio* (*On the Relationship Between Faith and Reason*) (Washington, DC: United States Conference of Catholic Bishops, 1998), no. 62.

disciplines.[95] This can be satisfied in the context of the college seminary program or the two-year pre-theology program.

153.　There is an "intimate bond which ties theological work to the philosophical search for truth."[96] It is essential that seminarians develop an understanding of the relationship between faith and reason and the relationship and interaction between philosophy and theology. "A proper philosophical training is vital, not only because of the links between the great philosophical questions and the mysteries of salvation which are studied in theology under the guidance of the higher light of faith, but also vis-à-vis an extremely widespread cultural situation which emphasizes subjectivism as a criterion and measure of truth: only a sound philosophy can help candidates for the priesthood to develop a reflective awareness of the fundamental relationship that exists between the human spirit and truth, that truth which is revealed to us fully in Jesus Christ" (*Pastores dabo vobis*, no. 52).

154.　The study of philosophy is not just part of intellectual formation, but is also connected to human, spiritual, and pastoral formation. Issues about priestly identity and the apostolic and missionary dimensions of priestly ministry "are closely linked to the question about the nature of truth." Philosophy serves "as a guarantee of that *certainty of truth* which is the only firm basis for a total giving of oneself to Jesus and to the Church" (*Pastores dabo vobis*, no. 52).

155.　The seminary philosophy program of studies should be balanced, comprehensive, integrated, and coherent. The philosophy program must include substantial studies in the history of philosophy treating ancient, medieval, modern, and contemporary philosophy.

- The study of the history of philosophy helps seminarians understand philosophical issues as they have developed in the Western philosophical tradition and, more particularly, in the Catholic intellectual tradition that has been both shaped by and contributed to the shape of the Western philosophical tradition. The knowledge of philosophy, with its powerful impact on theology

---

95　See CIC, c. 250; CCEO, c. 348§1.
96　*Fides et ratio*, no. 63.

and theologians, is necessary in order to appreciate the richness of our theological tradition.

- At the same time, it prepares seminarians for priestly ministry. By living more reflectively in the historical Catholic intellectual tradition, seminarians are better equipped for their ministry of teaching the faith and better prepared to engage contemporary culture, better prepared for the "evangelization of culture," which is integral to the new evangelization. In this regard, some treatment of American philosophy or social thought is also helpful for seminarians in understanding the dynamics of contemporary society in the United States.

156.   The philosophy program must include the study of logic, epistemology, philosophy of nature, metaphysics, natural theology, anthropology, and ethics:

- The study of logic helps seminarians to develop their critical and analytical abilities and become clearer thinkers who will be better able rationally to present, discuss, and defend the truths of the faith.
- The study of epistemology, the investigation of the nature and properties of knowledge, helps seminarians see "that human knowledge is capable of gathering from contingent reality objective and necessary truths,"[97] while recognizing also the limits of human knowledge. Moreover, it reinforces their understanding of the relationship between reason and revelation. They come to appreciate the power of reason to know the truth, and yet, as they confront the limits of the powers of human reason, they are opened to look to revelation for a fuller knowledge of those truths that exceed the power of human reason.
- The study of the philosophy of nature, which treats fundamental principles like substance, form, matter, causality, motion, and the soul, provides seminarians a foundation for the study of metaphysics, natural theology, anthropology, and ethics.
- The study of metaphysics helps seminarians explore fundamental issues concerning the nature of reality and see that reality and truth transcend the empirical. "A philosophy which shuns

---

97   Congregation for Catholic Education, *The Study of Philosophy in Seminaries* (1972).

metaphysics would be radically unsuited to the task of mediation in the understanding of revelation."[98] As the seminarian confronts the questions about the nature of being, he gains a deeper understanding and appreciation of God as the source of all being and gains some sense of how profound is this truth. A strong background in metaphysics also gives him the structure and ability to discuss certain theological concepts that depend on metaphysics for their articulation and explanation.

- The study of natural theology, which treats the existence of God *POG* and the attributes of God by means of the natural light of reason, provides a foundation for the seminarian's study of theology and the knowledge of God by means of revelation.

- The study of philosophical anthropology helps seminarians explore "the authentic spirituality of man, leading to a theocentric ethic, transcending earthly life, and at the same time open to the social dimension of man."[99] The philosophical study of "the human person, his fulfillment in intersubjectivity, his destiny, his inalienable rights, and his 'nuptial character' as one of the primary elements which is expressive of human nature and constitutive of society"[100] provides a foundation for the seminarian's study of theological anthropology.

- The study of ethics, which treats general principles of ethical decision making, provides seminarians with a solid grounding in themes like conscience, freedom, law, responsibility, virtue, and guilt. Ethics also considers the common good and virtue of solidarity as central to Christian social political philosophy. It provides a foundation for the seminarian's study of moral theology.

157.   "Philosophical instruction must be grounded in the perennially valid philosophical heritage and also take into account philosophical investigation over the course of time. It is to be taught in such a way that it perfects the human development of students, sharpens their minds, and makes them better able to pursue theological studies."[101] The philosophy of St. Thomas Aquinas should be given the recognition that the

---

98   *Fides et ratio*, no. 83.
99   *The Study of Philosophy in Seminaries.*
100   Congregation for Catholic Education, *Directives Regarding the Formation of Seminarians for Ministry to Marriage and Family* (1995), no. 21.
101   CIC, c. 251; cf. CCEO, c. 349§1.

Church accords it.[102] Especially in the courses on the history of philosophy, there should be a significant treatment of St. Thomas's thought, along with its ancient sources and its later development. The fruitful relationship between philosophy and theology in the Christian tradition should be explored through studies in Thomistic thought as well as that of other great Christian theologians who were also great philosophers. These include certain Fathers of the Church, medieval doctors, and recent Christian thinkers in the Western and Eastern traditions.[103]

Undergraduate Theology

Catholic Studies 201

158.   College-level seminarians should also begin the study of theology, with undergraduate courses that focus on the fundamental beliefs and practices of the Catholic faith. In particular, they should concentrate on those elements of the faith that may have been overlooked or neglected in the students' earlier religious education and that stand as a presupposition for all forms of graduate theological study. College-level theology courses should study the themes contained in the *Catechism of the Catholic Church*, including courses on Catholic doctrine, liturgy and sacraments, Catholic morality, Christian prayer, and Sacred Scripture. All seminarians should be thoroughly acquainted with the *Catechism of the Catholic Church* and its contents as a source for "a full, complete exposition of Catholic doctrine" and for "the requirements of contemporary catechetical instruction."[104]

159.   From the beginning, students should learn to relate theology to the larger mission of the Church in the public sphere. College-level theology courses are intended as preparation for studies in the theologate, not as a replacement for them.

---

102   See *Optatam totius*, no. 15; *Pastores dabo vobis*, no. 53; *Fides et ratio*, nos. 43-44; CIC, c. 251; CCEO, c. 349§1. In articulating the mind of the Fathers of the Second Vatican Council on this point, the Congregation for Catholic Education, in its document on *The Study of Philosophy in Seminaries*, observed that "the repeated recommendations of the Church about the philosophy of St. Thomas Aquinas remain fully justified and still valid. In this philosophy the first principles of natural truth are clearly and organically enunciated and harmonized with revelation. Within it also is enclosed that creative dynamism which, as biographers attest, marked the teaching of St. Thomas and which must also characterize the teaching of those who desire to follow his footsteps in a continual and renewed synthesizing of the valid conclusions received from tradition with new conquests of human thought."

103   See *Fides et ratio*, no. 74.

104   Pope John Paul II, *Laetamur magnopere* (in which the Latin Typical Edition of the *Catechism of the Catholic Church* Is Approved and Promulgated), in CCC.

Cultural Preparation Programs

160.   In some dioceses, international candidates have an opportunity to learn the English language and study United States culture as a prelude to their preparation for priestly ministry in a theologate in the United States. In addition to the study of United States history, culture, and language, these programs may also supplement the seminarians' college, philosophical, and even pastoral background as a preparation for graduate-level study of theology.

Pre-Theology

161.   Pre-theology programs, often organized in conjunction with a theologate or college seminary, prepare seminarians who have completed college but lack the philosophical and theological background and other areas necessary to pursue graduate-level theology. The study of philosophy is central to the academic formation of all pre-theology programs. The philosophical and theological preparation of pre-theology seminarians ought to match the requirements, as described above, for seminarians in a college seminary program, in particular, the 30 credit hours of philosophy. The temptation to abbreviate or circumvent requirements for pre-theology seminarians ought to be strenuously avoided.

162.   Besides philosophical and theological studies, the pre-theology program should strive to provide seminarians with an understanding of the historical and cultural context of their faith. Those who begin pre-theology without a solid liberal arts education should be provided a curriculum that supplies for lacunae in this area. The Catholic intellectual tradition (e.g., literature and the arts) should be a part of such a curriculum. Education in rhetoric and communications as well as language study is appropriate for a pre-theology course of studies. Latin and Greek are especially important. The study of Spanish or other languages used where one will serve in pastoral ministry should be included in the course of studies throughout the period of priestly formation, including pre-theology.

GRADUATE THEOLOGY

163.   Ultimately, intellectual formation in the seminary program centers on theology as a search for "an ever deeper knowledge of the divine mysteries" (*Pastores dabo vobis*, no. 51). This kind of theological study,

which far exceeds a purely technical approach to "religious phenomena," unfolds in the following ways:

Heart + Head combination (handwritten)

- Theology in seminary intellectual formation is truly to be *fides quaerens intellectum*, faith seeking understanding.[105] This direction is not the same as the approach of religious studies or the history of religions. The seminary study of theology begins in faith and ends in faith, as should all true theological inquiry and study.

- In a seminary or priestly formation context, the study of theology is oriented to one's own faith and also to the faith of others. In other words, the study of theology is apostolically motivated. "For the salvation of their brothers and sisters they should seek an ever deeper knowledge of the divine mysteries" (*Pastores dabo vobis*, no. 51). *Study for others → Not yourself* (handwritten)

- At the same time, this study of theology, as we have already noted, enriches and expands the personal faith of the seminarian studying it.[106]

- When theology is studied in the context of priestly formation, it cannot be detached from other human knowledge. In fact, it is to be integrated with other elements of human understanding, especially philosophy and the human sciences.[107] *Catholic Studies* (handwritten)

- The seminary study of theology, because it begins in faith and ends in faith, must also flow from prayer and lead to prayer.[108]

- In a particular way, the theology studied in preparation for priestly ministry must find integration and focus in the liturgy, the celebration of the Mystery of Christ.

- Because theology studied in light of priestly mission and ministry must be directed to a practical wisdom, it must offer a complete and unified vision of the truths of faith.[109] This wisdom and unified vision, then, is something that can be conveyed in the priest's preaching, that allows him to bring the Word of God into dialogue with the contemporary human situation.[110]

---

105 See *Pastores dabo vobis*, no. 53.
106 See *Pastores dabo vobis*, no. 53.
107 See *Pastores dabo vobis*, no. 53.
108 See *Pastores dabo vobis*, no. 54.
109 See *Pastores dabo vobis*, no. 54.
110 See United States Conference of Catholic Bishops, *Fulfilled in Your Hearing: The Homily in the Sunday Assembly* (Washington, DC: United States Conference of Catholic Bishops, 1982), 13.

- Because theology is rooted in the Church's faith and serves the faith of the Church, it must be studied in complete and faithful communion with the Magisterium.[111]
- Theology studied in a seminary and destined to contribute to the mission of the Church through priestly ministry must necessarily be concerned about restoring Christian unity. Theological studies must impart an adequate grasp of the Catholic principles on ecumenism.[112] The ecumenical imperative that flows from the prayer of Christ for his flock and the renewed vision of the Second Vatican Council demand this focus.
- Theology's theoretical and practical dimensions in priestly mission and ministry mean that it must be rigorous both academically and pastorally in its orientation.[113]
- Finally, the study of theology must be an initiation into a lifelong study of the truths of faith. If the priest is to be a teacher, he must first be a student who continuously pursues an understanding of the faith to which he commits himself and invites his people.

INTEGRATION OF INTELLECTUAL FORMATION WITH THE OTHER PILLARS

164.   Intellectual formation is closely related to the other three pillars of formation. As it develops the gift of human intelligence and so enables it to be in service to one's brothers and sisters in faith, intellectual formation complements and guides human formation. Intellectual formation applies not only to a comprehensive understanding of the mysteries of the Catholic faith, but also to an ability to explain and even defend the reasoning that supports those truths. In this way, it provides those who are being formed spiritually with a knowledge of the Lord and his ways which they embrace in faith. Finally, intellectual formation through the study of theology enables priests to contemplate, share, and communicate the mysteries of faith with others. In this way, it has an essentially pastoral orientation.

---

111   See *Pastores dabo vobis*, no. 55.
112   See Second Vatican Council, *Unitatis redintegratio* (*Decree on Ecumenism*) (1964), nos. 2-4.
113   See *Pastores dabo vobis*, nos. 55-56.

NORMS FOR INTELLECTUAL FORMATION

Intellectual Formation—High School Seminaries: Norms

165.   A well-organized and comprehensive academic curriculum, staffed by competent teachers, is essential.

166.   Proper resources and adequate facilities for students and faculty to achieve the ends of sound secondary education should be provided.

167.   The linguistic and cultural situation of the students must be taken into consideration in planning and executing the curriculum.

168.   The program should provide for the special needs of students of varied cultural heritages.

169.   The very reason for their existence presumes that high school seminaries offer an excellent curriculum of religious instruction. In addition to the major themes of the *Catechism of the Catholic Church*, these programs should provide courses in Church history and Catholic social teaching. The goal of this catechesis is to engage the young student in a personal relationship with the Lord Jesus and call forth a deep commitment to his mission and message to the world.

170.   High school seminary religion courses should use only those texts found to be in conformity with the *Catechism of the Catholic Church* (by the USCCB Ad Hoc Committee for the Implementation of the *Catechism*).

171.   High school seminaries must require a classic college preparatory program. This program should include English, literature, world and American history, mathematics, science, speech, government, music, and art.

172.   The study of Latin and Greek represents a valuable component in a serious high school education and is strongly advised. The study of modern languages, especially Spanish, is also strongly advised. For international seminarians, proficiency with the English language is to be encouraged at this level, along with familiarity of United States culture.

173.   Academic counseling should be provided in light of college seminary requirements and entrance prerequisites.

174.   High school seminaries must have a fully accredited academic program.

Intellectual Formation—College Seminaries: Norms

175.   College seminarians should earn a bachelor of arts degree from their accredited college seminary. If such a degree is not available from their college seminary, they may earn the degree at a college or university associated with the seminary.

176.   A college seminary program must offer courses in philosophy and undergraduate theology or provide for them at a Catholic college or university that possesses a complete curriculum of philosophical and theological studies.

177.   Philosophy and theology teachers in college seminaries are expected to make a profession of faith and have a canonical mission.[114]

178.   Sound philosophical formation requires a biennium of study, which is understood in the United States to be at least 30 semester credit hours,[115] together with the out-of-classroom work associated with each credit hour traditionally expected in American higher education. The philosophical curriculum must include the study of the history of philosophy (ancient, medieval, modern, and contemporary), logic, epistemology, metaphysics, philosophy of nature, natural theology, anthropology and ethics.

179.   A minimum of 12 semester credit hours must be required in appropriate courses of undergraduate theology. These courses should study the themes of the Catechism (doctrine, liturgy and sacraments, morality, prayer) as well as Sacred Scripture.

180.   The academic dean and ultimately the rector should be vigilant that the philosophical and theological instruction received at a college/

---

114   See CIC, c. 833, 6°.
115   See *Pastores dabo vobis*, no. 56, and *Fides et ratio*, no. 62.

university is consistent with magisterial teaching and the requirements as stated in this *Program of Priestly Formation.*

181.   Programs that utilize colleges and universities for philosophy and theological studies should carefully and consistently monitor the content and quality of those courses. It is essential that philosophical instruction be grounded in the perennially valid philosophical heritage, as well as take into account philosophical investigation over the course of time.[116]

182.   The curriculum of studies of college seminarians must include a grounding in the liberal arts and sciences, including studies in the humanities. Special attention is to be given to classical and foreign languages. A knowledge of Latin and the biblical languages is foundational and should be given the emphasis that the Church accords it.[117] Particular attention must be given to ensure that before entering the theologate all seminarians can demonstrate that they have acquired that "knowledge of Latin which will enable them to understand and make use of so many scientific sources and of the documents of the Church," according to the insistence of the Fathers of the Second Vatican Council.[118] The study of the Spanish language and Hispanic cultures as well as other pastorally appropriate languages and cultures is recommended. In some cases, an English Language Program (ELP) may form an important part of the program. Since preaching is at the heart of priestly ministry, college seminaries should include courses in writing and speech.

183.   Educational standards should not be so rigid or restrictive as to close the door to candidates who are lacking in some dimension of the required educational background. Remedial help should be provided to such students so that their academic deficiencies may be overcome.

184.   Excellence in education at the college level demands access to a strong library with print, non-print, and electronic resources, that is professionally staffed, as required by accrediting agencies.

---

116   See CIC, c. 251; CCEO, c. 349§1.
117   See *Optatam totius*, no. 13; CIC, c. 249.
118   *Optatam totius*, no. 13.

Intellectual Formation—Pre-Theology: Norms

185.   Because two full years should be dedicated to the philosophical disciplines,[119] pre-theology programs should extend for at least two calendar years in length.

186.   Sound philosophical formation requires a biennium of study, which is understood in the United States to be at least 30 semester credit hours[120] together with the out-of-classroom work associated with each credit hour traditionally expected in American higher education. The philosophical curriculum must include the study of the history of philosophy (ancient, medieval, modern, and contemporary), logic, epistemology, metaphysics, philosophy of nature, natural theology, anthropology, and ethics. Seminaries should ensure that the philosophy is appropriate for studying Catholic theology and explore creative curricular strategies so that students can grasp the linkage between philosophical insights and theological frameworks.

187.   A minimum of 12 semester credit hours is required in appropriate courses of undergraduate theology, which provide a solid foundation in Catholic doctrine through a thorough study of the *Catechism of the Catholic Church*. These courses should study the themes of the Catechism (doctrine, liturgy and sacraments, morality, prayer) as well as Sacred Scripture.

188.   Programs that utilize colleges and universities for philosophy and theological studies should carefully and consistently monitor the content and quality of their students' courses. It is essential that philosophical instruction be grounded in the perennially valid philosophical heritage, as well as taking into account philosophical investigations over the course of time.[121]

189.   A knowledge of Latin and the biblical languages is foundational and should be given the emphasis that church teaching accords it.[122] Particular attention must be given to ensure that before entering the theologate all seminarians can demonstrate that they have acquired

---

119   See CIC, c. 250; CCEO, c. 348§1.
120   See *Pastores dabo vobis*, no. 56, and *Fides et ratio*, no. 62.
121   See CIC, c. 251; CCEO, c. 349.
122   See *Optatam totius*, no. 13; CIC, c. 249.

that "knowledge of Latin which will enable them to understand and make use of the sources of so many sciences and the documents of the Church," according to the insistence of the Fathers of the Second Vatican Council.[123] The study of Spanish should also be encouraged. Facility with other liturgical and spoken languages may be necessary for those of the Eastern Churches.

190.   Paralleling other levels of intellectual formation, pre-theology programs are encouraged to consider offering the civilly-recognized bachelor in philosophy (PhB), a two-year degree program, which presumes a previous bachelor's degree (preferably in the liberal arts), but does not require a liberal arts component. Such a degree requires regional accreditation.

Intellectual Formation—Theologates: Norms

191.   At least four full years should be dedicated to graduate theological studies.

192.   Graduate theological studies require an appropriate and sound philosophical formation. Those requirements, identified in the norms on college seminaries and pre-theology programs, are prerequisite for theological studies (see also nos. 34 to 67 of this document, on admissions).

193.   Teachers of theology in seminaries are expected to make a profession of faith and have a canonical mission.[124]

194.   The academic curriculum as a whole should have a discernible and coherent unity.

195.   The curriculum must reflect the specialized nature of priestly formation and assist seminarians in developing a clear understanding of the ministerial priesthood.

196.   Due consideration should be given in theological formation to its pastoral aim. Theological studies should be designed with the pastoral goal in view, recognizing that the pastoral character of priestly

---

123   *Optatam totius*, no. 13.
124   See CIC, c. 833, 6°.

formation applies to intellectual formation as well as to the other areas of formation.[125]

197.   The core should include fundamental theology, the basis of the rational procedure of all theology and, thus, the introduction to the study of theology.[126]

198.   The various theological disciplines should recognize Sacred Scripture as foundational and as the point of departure and soul of all theology. [127]

199.   In Scripture, the core should include the study of the Pentateuch, the historical, prophetic and wisdom (especially the Psalms) books of the Old Testament, the Synoptic Gospels and Acts, Pauline and Johannine literature, and the Catholic epistles.

200.   The proper understanding of Sacred Scripture requires the use of the historical-critical method, though this method is not totally sufficient. Other methods that are synchronic in approach are helpful in bringing forth the riches contained in the biblical texts.[128] The study of Scripture and its interpretation should take into account the preparation of seminarians for the tasks of preaching homilies and applying Scripture to the lives of the Christian faithful.[129]

201.   Patristic studies constitute an essential part of theological studies. Theology should draw from the works of the Fathers of the Church that have lasting value within the living tradition of the Church. The core should include patrology (an overview of the life and writings of the Fathers of the Church) and patristics (an overview of the theological thought of the Fathers of the Church).[130]

---

125   See *Pastores dabo vobis*, nos. 55, 57.
126   See Sacred Congregation for Catholic Education, *The Theological Formation of Future Priests* (1976), nos. 107-113.
127   See Second Vatican Council, *Dei verbum* (*Dogmatic Constitution on Divine Revelation*) (1965), no. 24; CCC, no. 113; CIC, c. 252§2; CCEO, c. 350§2; *The Theological Formation of Future Priests*, no. 79.
128   See Pontifical Biblical Commission, *The Interpretation of the Bible in the Church* (1993).
129   Because "in the sacred books the Father who is in heaven comes lovingly to meet his children, and talks with them," courses in Sacred Scripture must equip seminarians to identify those "divinely revealed realities, which are contained and presented [therein]" (*Dei verbum*, nos. 21, 11), so that they can share these riches with those they serve.
130   See Congregation for Catholic Education, *Instruction on the Study of the Fathers of the Church in the Formation of Priests* (1989).

202.   In dogmatic theology, the core must include theology of God, One and Three, Christology, Creation, the Fall and the nature of sin, redemption, grace and the human person, ecclesiology, sacraments, eschatology, Mariology,[131] and missiology.[132] A separate course on Holy Orders, with a thorough study of the nature and mission of the ministerial priesthood including a history and theology of celibacy, is required.

203.   The Church enjoins pastors "to neglect nothing with a view to a well-organized and well-oriented catechetical effort" and, since "all pastors have a duty to provide it," evangelization and catechesis should have a prominent place in the seminary curriculum.[133] A sound study of the content and methods of catechesis not only prepares the seminarian for his task as a minister of the Word, but also provides the possibility of a synthetic moment in the curriculum when an integrated unity can be brought to his years of theological study.[134]

204.   In moral theology, the core must include fundamental moral theology, medical-moral ethics, sexual morality, and social ethics.

205.   Moral theology should be taught in a way that draws deeply from Sacred Scripture and Tradition, refers to the natural law and absolute moral norms, and gives consideration to the results of the natural and human sciences. The close link between moral, spiritual, and dogmatic theology should be evident. The pastoral task of priests as ministers of the Sacrament of Penance should also be kept in mind in the teaching of moral theology.[135]

206.   The importance of a clear grasp of the principles of medical-moral ethics cannot be underestimated for the future priest in the contemporary culture. Special attention during his preparation should be given to the fundamental respect for human life from conception to natural death and to the moral evils of and pastoral means of addressing contraception, abortion, and euthanasia.

---

131 See Congregation for Catholic Education, *The Virgin Mary in Intellectual and Spiritual Formation* (1988).
132 Missiology may be treated as a separate component or integrated into ecclesiology; it must form an integral part of every treatment of evangelization.
133 John Paul II, *Catechesi tradendae* (*On Catechesis in Our Time*) (Washington, DC: United States Conference of Catholic Bishops, 1979), no. 64.
134 See *Optatam totius*, no. 19; CIC, cc. 254 and 256; CCEO, c. 352§§2-3.
135 See *Optatam totius*, no. 16; *The Theological Formation of Future Priests*, 95-101; *Veritatis splendor*, no. 95.

207.   The teaching of sexual ethics must be thorough and unambiguous in its presentation of the authentic teaching of the Church in sexual moral matters—presuming a mature biological and basic social scientific understanding of human sexuality. This is a matter of special import since the seminarian's formation in celibate chastity includes the intellectual assent to, and embrace of, the Church's moral teachings in matters of sexuality.

208.   The social teaching of the Church must be presented in its entirety with appropriate principles of reflection, criteria for judgment, and norms for action. The systematic study of the social encyclicals of the popes is especially recommended.[136]

209.   Adequate instruction must be given in professional ethics appropriate to priesthood and priestly ministry.

210.   In historical studies, the core should include courses on the history of the Church universal and the history of the Catholic Church in the United States that would be taught in a way which reflects her multicultural origins and ecumenical context. Among historical studies, the study of patristics and the lives of the saints are of special importance.

211.   In canon law, the core should include a general introduction to canon law and the canon law of individual sacraments, including but not limited to the Sacrament of Matrimony. Additional courses in canon law, particularly on Books II ("The People of God") and V ("The Temporal Goods of the Church") of the Code of Canon Law, and Titles I ("The Rights and Obligations of All the Christian Faithful"), VII ("Eparchies and Bishops"), X ("Clerics"), and XXIII ("The Temporal Goods of the Church") of the Code of Canons of the Eastern Churches, would assist seminarians in preparing for their pastoral ministry.[137]

212.   Studies in spirituality and spiritual direction are to be included. Spirituality studies the Catholic spiritual tradition, provides practical directives for the Christian call to perfection, and proposes principles of discernment for individual as well as group spiritual experiences. This

---

136   See Congregation for Catholic Education, Guidelines for the Study and Teaching of the Church's Social Doctrine in the Formation of Priests (1988).
137   See CIC, c. 256§1; CCEO, c. 352§§2-3; Congregation for Catholic Education, On the Teaching of Canon Law to Those Preparing to Be Priests (1975).

study should also explore the spirituality of various vocations, especially the priesthood and consecrated life. Spiritual direction teaches the art of fostering the spiritual life of those entrusted to one's care.

213.   In liturgy, the core should include studies in the theological, historical, spiritual, pastoral, and juridical aspects of liturgy.[138]

214.   Seminarians must learn to celebrate all of the Church's sacred rites according to the mind of the Church, without addition or subtraction. Liturgical practica should include the celebration of the Eucharist and the other sacraments, with particular attention given to the practicum for the Sacrament of Penance. Seminarians should be introduced to the official liturgical books used by the clergy and to the Church's directives for music, art, and architecture.[139]

215.   Homiletics should occupy a prominent place in the core curriculum and be integrated into the entire course of studies. In addition to the principles of biblical interpretation, catechesis, and communications theory, seminarians should also learn the practical skills needed to communicate the Gospel as proclaimed by the Church in an effective and appropriate manner. Seminarians should be taught that "through the course of the liturgical year, the homily sets forth the mysteries of faith and the standards of the Christian life on the basis of the sacred text."[140] Seminarians should also be afforded opportunities to preach outside of Eucharistic celebrations and receive proper assessment. Where appropriate, seminarians should be able to demonstrate a capacity for bilingual preaching.

216.   The core should include an introductory course in ecumenism that treats the Catholic Church's commitment to the principles of ecumenism, the fundamental role of ecumenical dialogue, and current ecumenical issues. In addition, ecumenism should be fully integrated into other courses, thus permeating the theological curriculum. Issues concerning interreligious dialogue also should be discussed. Particularly important is an awareness of the world religions and their relationship to Christianity. This is especially true of Judaism, Islam, and certain Asian religions.

---

138   See Congregation for Catholic Education, *Instruction on Liturgical Formation in Seminaries* (1979).
139   See *Ecclesia de Eucharistia*, no. 5; *General Instruction of the Roman Missal*, nos. 5-6.
140   *Praenotanda* of the *Lectionary for the Mass* (1981).

217.   Studies in pastoral theology are required and should include treatment of the principles and criteria for pastoral action and provide for theological reflection where seminarians are involved in supervised pastoral placements.[141] Pastoral studies should include training in pastoral counseling, where seminarians are to learn how to address concerns brought to them by parishioners for whom they can reasonably offer counsel and how to make appropriate referrals for issues beyond their competence.

218.   Due emphasis should be given in the various theological disciplines to the topic of marriage and the family. There should be interdisciplinary cooperation, and the curriculum should be organized so that the topic of the family becomes an important dimension of pastoral and intellectual formation.[142]

219.   Although various theological schools exist within the Catholic tradition, in accord with church teaching, the significance of St. Thomas Aquinas as the model and guide for study and research in theology should be recognized.[143]

220.   Throughout the academic curriculum, questions of theological methodology should be emphasized so that students learn to evaluate the strengths and limitations of various theological viewpoints in light of the Magisterium of the Church.

221.   All methodologies employed must be clear on the distinction and relation between truths revealed by God and contained in the deposit of faith, and their theological mode of expression.[144]

222.   The normative function of the Magisterium must be presented as Christ's gift to his Church: the vital, integral, and authoritative voice in the theological enterprise.

223.   Courses in theology, history, and liturgy, where appropriate, should include the role and contribution of the Eastern Churches.[145]

---

141   See *Pastores dabo vobis*, no. 57; *The Theological Formation of Future Priests*, nos. 102-106.
142   See Congregation for Catholic Education, *Directives on the Formation of Seminarians Concerning Problems Related to Marriage and the Family* (1995).
143   See *Optatam totius*, no. 16; CIC, c. 252§3.
144   See International Theological Commission, *On the Interpretation of Dogmas* (1989).
145   See Congregation for Catholic Education, *Circular Letter Concerning Studies of the Oriental Churches* (1987).

224. Studies in the belief and practices of other churches, ecclesial communities, or religions may be profitably taught by members of those churches or religions after students have completed the regular course studies on ecclesiology and the Catholic principles on ecumenism, and with respect for the rule that in seminary studies professors of the doctrinal courses should be Catholics.[146] The prescriptions of the *Directory for the Application of Principles and Norms on Ecumenism* (nos. 70-81, 192-195) are to be followed.

225. Theological formation in seminaries must clearly respect traditional doctrinal formulations of the faith while recognizing contemporary modes of theological expression and explanation.

226. Theological education for the priesthood should resist any tendency to reduce theology to a merely historical, sociological investigation or a comparative study of religions.

227. The entire academic program should be taught in such a way that it makes seminarians aware that they have a responsibility to continue their theological and pastoral education after ordination.

228. The theological curriculum, both in its planning and its execution, should address the unique needs of a multicultural society. The study of the Spanish language and Hispanic cultures as well as other pastorally appropriate languages and cultures is essential for most dioceses and is strongly recommended for all seminarians.[147]

229. Throughout the curriculum, the biblical, theological, ethical, and historical foundations of the Church's teaching on social justice should be highlighted.[148]

230. Seminarians should receive an introduction to the principles, methods, and skills of catechesis and teaching. Teaching opportunities may be offered as a part of field education and pastoral placements.

---

146 See Pontifical Council for Promoting Christian Unity, *Directory for the Application of Principles and Norms on Ecumenism* (1992).

147 See United States Conference of Catholic Bishops, *Encuentro and Mission: A Renewed Pastoral Framework for Hispanic Ministry* (Washington, DC: United States Conference of Catholic Bishops, 2002), 55.

148 See Pontifical Council for Justice and Peace, *Compendium of the Social Teaching of the Church* (Washington, DC: United States Conference of Catholic Bishops, 2005).

231.   In the United States, the first professional degree, master of divinity, is the recognized standard for preparation of students for ordained ministry across the broad spectrum of institutions of graduate theological education. Its curriculum incorporates the requirements of the *Program of Priestly Formation*. Seminaries in the United States whenever possible should offer a master of arts degree in theology to provide a deeper understanding of the theological disciplines for general educational purposes or for further graduate study. In addition, seminaries are also encouraged to offer the ecclesiastical degrees of bachelor in theology (STB) and the licentiate in theology (STL) either by affiliating with an ecclesiastical faculty or by special arrangement with the Congregation for Catholic Education.

232.   Seminaries ought to have degree programs certified by appropriate accrediting agencies. Students should not be excused from pursuing such degrees except for serious reasons. A seminarian is normally expected to obtain the master of divinity and/or the STB degree prior to ordination.

233.   As an essential resource for seminarians' life of study and reflection, the library collection of books and periodicals should be carefully maintained and appropriately expanded. Excellence in education at the theology level demands access to a strong, professionally staffed library with print, non-print, and electronic resources, as required by accrediting agencies.

234.   Contemporary pedagogical methods that incorporate technological advances should be encouraged.

235.   Diocesan bishops and religious ordinaries should be encouraged to designate students who complete their basic program with honors for further study after sufficient pastoral experience.

IV. PASTORAL FORMATION

236.   All four pillars of formation are interwoven and go forward concurrently. Still, in a certain sense, pastoral formation is the culmination of the entire formation process: "The whole formation imparted to candidates for the priesthood aims at preparing them to enter into communion with the charity of Christ the Good Shepherd. Hence, their formation in its different aspects must have a fundamentally pastoral character" (*Pastores dabo vobis*, no. 57).

In Persona Christi

237.   In virtue of the grace of Holy Orders, a priest is able to stand and act in the community in the name and person of Jesus Christ, Head and Shepherd of the Church. This sacramental character needs to be completed by the personal and pastoral formation of the priest, who appropriates "the mind of Christ" and effectively communicates the mysteries of faith through his human personality as a bridge, through his personal witness of faith rooted in his spiritual life, and through his knowledge of faith. These elements of formation converge in pastoral formation.

238.   The basic principle of pastoral formation is enunciated in *Pastores dabo vobis*, no. 57, in its citation of *Optatam totius*, no. 4: "The whole training of the students should have as its object to make them *true shepherds of souls after the example of our Lord Jesus Christ, teacher, priest, and shepherd.*" To be a true "shepherd of souls" means standing with and for Christ in the community, the Christ who teaches and sanctifies and guides or leads the community. The grace to be a shepherd comes with ordination. That grace, however, calls for the priest's personal commitment to develop the knowledge and skills to teach and preach well, to celebrate the sacraments both properly and prayerfully, and to respond to people's needs as well as to take initiatives in the community that holy leadership requires.

The same problem you have 5 mins before ordination.

239.   The aim of pastoral formation—the formation of a "true shepherd" who teaches, sanctifies, and governs or leads—implies that such formation must include a number of essential elements:

- *Proclamation of the Word*: Pastoral formation needs to emphasize the proclamation of God's Word, which indeed is the first task of the priest.[149] This proclamation ministry is aimed at the conversion of sinners and is rooted in the seminarian/preacher's ability to listen deeply to the lived experiences and realities of the faithful. This listening is followed by the preacher's ability to interpret those lived experiences in the light of Sacred Scripture and the Church's Tradition.[150] Understanding this intersection of God's Word and human experiences, the seminarian/preacher initiates a lifelong mission and ministry of bringing God's Word to the world through preaching and teaching. This requires that the seminarian couple the deepest convictions of faith with the

---

149   See *Presbyterorum ordinis*, no. 4.
150   See *Fulfilled in Your Hearing*, 20.

→ Pub speaking

development of his communication skills so that God's Word may be effectively expressed.

- *The sacramental dimension*: The celebration of the sacraments is central to the priest's ministry. Although the seminarian cannot celebrate the sacraments as a priest does, he can accompany priests who do and he can prepare those who participate in them. In this way, he begins to have a sense of what his sacramental ministry will entail. He will come to appreciate the sacraments as part of his future public ministry for the salvation of souls and understand more clearly how the Church's sacraments, especially the Eucharist, nourish and sustain God's people.

- *The missionary dimension*: All priests are to have the heart of missionaries.[151] The Church is truest to her identity when she is an evangelizing Church. This is because the very nature of the Church is missionary.[152] Seminarians should be given an opportunity to become acquainted with the work of the Pontifical Mission Societies, the Missionary Congregations of Religious, the home missions, and the missionary tradition over the centuries. An exposure to the Church's missionary work during the years of formation can be beneficial to the seminarian, his discernment, and his future ministry.

- *The community dimension*: Pastoral formation must initiate seminarians to the care, guidance, and leadership that are extended to a community. The pastor is to be a man of communion and shepherd of a flock. In the United States context of individualism, the concern is that "pastoral formation" and "pastoral care" might otherwise be limited to one-to-one contact. Pastoral ministry is primarily directed to a community and then to individuals within that community.

- *Skills for effective public ministry*: Seminarians need to learn how to make available in service to God's people all the formation that has preceded (the human, the spiritual, and the intellectual). This means the acquisition of certain skills, for example, an ability to communicate the mysteries of faith in clear and readily comprehensible language[153] using media appropriate to the social context. At the same time, pastoral formation means more than

---

151   See *Redemptoris missio*, no. 67.
152   See Second Vatican Council, *Ad gentes divinitus* (*Decree on the Church's Missionary Activity*), no. 2.
153   See CIC, c. 255; CCEO, c. 352§2.

acquiring skills. It signifies a level of personal development, fitting for a priest who acts in the person of Jesus Christ, Head and Shepherd of the Church. Effective public ministry means, for example, the cultivation of a flexibility of spirit that enables the priest to relate to people across a number of different cultures and theological and ecclesial outlooks. Formation must help the seminarian put on both the mind and heart of Christ, the Good Shepherd.[154]

- *A personal synthesis for practical use*: Another way of viewing pastoral formation is to see it as a process linking the elements of human, spiritual, and intellectual formation in such a way that they can be put to practical use for others, especially in a parish context.[155] In a parish internship experience, for example, the seminarian draws on the experience before him in the parish and asks how his human, spiritual, and intellectual formation makes a difference. With due attention to the disciplines of the Church, preaching might be one instance of a theoretical, personal, and practical synthesis. In this and other ways, he revisits his formation and views it through the lens of practice, application, and impact.

- *An initiation to various practical, pastoral experiences, especially in parishes*: It is important not to sacrifice human, spiritual, and intellectual formation for practical experience. Still, it is essential to cultivate pastoral formation and to enhance and integrate the other dimensions of formation so that the seminarian has opportunities to experience pastoral life firsthand.[156] Seminaries have initiated students into pastoral experiences and reflection on them in a variety of ways: concurrent field placements, pastoral quarters or internships, clinical pastoral education, and diaconate internships. Whatever the setting, it is necessary that it facilitate learning. It is also necessary that there be a guide, mentor, or teacher who accompanies the student and helps him to learn from the experience. In addition, there should be a priest supervisor who helps the student enter into the specifically priestly dimension of the ministry.[157] In these experiences,

---

154   See *Pastores dabo vobis*, no. 58.
155   See *Pastores dabo vobis*, no. 58.
156   See *Pastores dabo vobis*, no. 58.
157   See CIC, c. 258; CCEO, c. 353.

the student first enters the scene as an observer, then raises questions to understand what is happening, and finally relates it to his other formation. He ought then to practice or try to do what the situation requires. After that, he can profit from supervision that helps him to assess what happened and gives him feedback. A process of theological reflection follows that identifies the faith assumptions and convictions underlying both the situation and the ministerial response. Theological reflection thus provides an opportunity for personal synthesis, the clarification of motivations, and the development of directions for life and ministry. And the final step, of course, is in fact to return to the ministry or pastoral situation, but now with more knowledge and ability and a better inner sense of direction because of an enriched spiritual life and a more deeply grounded sense of priestly identity. It is the responsibility of the diocesan bishop, religious ordinary, and the rectors to ensure that the Catholic, sacramental dimension of pastoral care is integral to all such programs in which seminarians participate.

- *Cultural sensitivity*: Pastoral formation must flow from and move towards an appreciation of the multifaceted reality of the Church.[158] In the United States, this means a genuine appreciation of the diversity that marks the Catholic Church as well as the diversity that typifies this society generally. Seminarians need exposure to the many cultures and languages that belong to the Catholic Church in the United States. They should know how to welcome migrants and refugees pastorally, liturgically, and culturally. Simultaneously, they should assist newcomers to adapt themselves into the mainstream without each one losing their own identity.[159]

- *Religious pluralism*: They also need to know, appreciate, and learn how to work within the ecumenical and interfaith context that forms a backdrop for life in the United States and for the Catholic Church in this nation.

- *Formation for a particular presbyterate and a local Church*: All pastoral formation must be profoundly ecclesial in nature. One of its principal aims is the familiarization of seminarians with the

---

158   See *Pastores dabo vobis*, no. 59.
159   See Pontifical Council for the Pastoral Care of Migrants and Itinerant People, *Erga migrantes* (*Instruction on the Love of Christ Towards Migrants*) (2004).

local Church that they will serve and especially the priests with whom they will be co-workers with the bishop. This dimension of pastoral formation not only means absorbing information about the local Church and presbyterate, but, more importantly, cultivating bonds of affective communion and learning how to be at home in the place where one will serve and with the priests with whom one will serve. Seminarians should see their future priestly assignments as something wider than their own preference and choice, but rather as a sharing in a far wider vision of the needs of the local Church.

- *The poor*: If seminarians are to be formed after the model of Jesus, the Good Shepherd, who came "to bring glad tidings to the poor," then they must have sustained contact with those who are privileged in God's eyes—the poor, the marginalized, the sick, and the suffering. In the course of these encounters, they learn to cultivate a preferential option for the poor. They also need to become aware of the social contexts and structures that can breed injustice as well as ways of promoting more just contexts and structures.

- *Leadership development*: Pastoral formation means that seminarians learn how to take spiritual initiatives and direct a community into action or movement. That leadership also includes a dimension of practical administration. The pastoral formation program should provide opportunities for seminarians to acquire the basic administrative skills necessary for effective pastoral leadership, recognizing that programs of continuing education and ongoing formation will be necessary to equip newly ordained priests to assume future responsibilities as pastors. Additional leadership skills include an ability to manage the physical and financial resources of the parish, including educating parishioners about the gospel value of stewardship, and an ability to organize parochial life effectively to achieve the goals of the new evangelization.

- *The cultivation of personal qualities*: In the current situation in the United States, parish life is blessed with many people who serve—permanent deacons, men and women religious, professional lay ministers, volunteers, and members of parish and diocesan consultative bodies. To direct others and to work well with them, priests need a number of personal qualities. A seminarian who aspires to serve as a priest needs to cultivate these qualities in the process of pastoral formation. They include a sense of responsibility for initiating and completing tasks, a spirit of collaboration with others, an ability to facilitate resolution of conflicts, a flexibility of spirit that is able to make adjustments for new and unexpected circumstances, an availability to those who serve and those who are served, and, finally, zeal—or the ardent desire to bring all people closer to the Lord.

240. Pastoral formation depends in great measure on the quality of supervision. To serve as a supervisor of seminarians calls for experience, competence, and generosity. Priests and others who serve as supervisors, mentors, and teachers are an extension of the faculty of the seminary. It is important that this identification with priestly formation become part of the mindset of pastoral staffs that serve to initiate seminarians to pastoral life. When onsite pastoral formation is seen as an integral part of priestly formation, then pastoral staffs must accept a special responsibility in the name of the Church for the direction and help they provide to seminarians. These priests and those associated with them must have certain qualities that include loyal commitment to priestly formation, patience, honesty, an almost instinctive way of thinking theologically in pastoral situations, and a habit of prayer that permeates the ministry.

241. Clearly, pastoral formation not only connects with the other three pillars of priestly formation, but in itself it provides a goal that integrates the other dimensions. Human formation enables priests to be bridges to communicate Jesus Christ, a pastoral function. Spiritual formation enables priests to persevere in and give depth to their ministry. Intellectual formation provides criteria and content to ensure that pastoral efforts are directed correctly, properly, and effectively.

Pastoral is all the pillars compared

NORMS FOR PASTORAL FORMATION

242. Every seminary is required to offer a coordinated program of pastoral formation that forms candidates for the priesthood who are able to support men and women in answering the universal call to holiness.[160]

---

160 See *Lumen gentium*, section V.

243.   The pastoral formation program should be an integral part of the seminary curriculum and accredited as such, but none of its elements should compromise the two years of full-time pre-theology studies or the four years of full-time theological studies.

244.   The goals and objectives of the pastoral formation program should be clearly stated and serve as the basis for the evaluation of seminarians in this area. This statement should also include a description of professional ministerial ethics.

245.   The director of pastoral formation should be a priest with faculty status, possess the requisite parochial experience and professional expertise, and participate in professional organizations in the area of seminary pastoral formation. The director should model a love for priestly ministry in the Church.

246.   The pastoral formation program should provide seminarians with a broad exposure to supervised pastoral service, with primary emphasis on parish ministry.

247.   Determinations about the concurrent or intensive residency (onsite) program should be made by the seminary in collaboration with the dioceses or religious institutes or societies it serves. Seminaries and dioceses that make provision for onsite experiences are also responsible for ensuring that these experiences help seminarians develop skills and attitudes that will enhance their future priestly ministry and that, when ecumenical in nature, for example, CPE, are respectful of the Catholic teaching, especially on moral or ethical issues. It is the responsibility of the diocesan bishop, religious ordinary, and the rectors to ensure that the Catholic, sacramental dimension of pastoral care is integral to all such programs in which seminarians participate.

248.   Supervision, theological reflection, and evaluation are necessary components of an effective pastoral program. Although theological reflection can help the development of pastoral skills, its primary purpose is to interpret pastoral experience or activity in light of Scripture, church teaching, personal faith, and pastoral practices. Reflection of this kind should become a lifelong habit in priestly ministry.

249.   Onsite supervisors should be carefully selected with an eye to their dedication to the Church and respect for the priesthood. They should be taught the skills of pastoral supervision and evaluation. In choosing pastoral internships and summer placements and their supervisors, bishops and vocation personnel should consider carefully the particular needs of individual seminarians and the available time and supervisory skills of the supervisors.

250.   In addition to onsite supervisors, others collaborating in the various ministries, as well as those served, should be asked to participate in the evaluation of seminarians in ministry.

251.   The pastoral formation program should provide the seminarians with experience in working with and for the poor. Participation in ecumenical and interreligious programs of social action and outreach is also helpful.

252.   The program should include placements in which seminarians will experience the richness and diversity of the various cultural, racial, and ethnic groups that compose the Catholic Church in the United States. Such placements can also provide opportunities to sharpen language skills.

253.   However the pastoral formation program is organized, it must pay attention to the seminarians' need to root a life of service in personal prayer. Seminarians need supervision in developing the habit of prayer in the context of pastoral activity and in learning to establish a rhythm of life that provides an appropriate balance of prayer, service, study, exercise, and leisure. Priest-supervisors and mentors should be chosen who model this balance in their own life and ministry. Evaluation of seminarians in ministerial placements should include observations leading to a growing accountability in these areas.

254.   The seminary should attempt to keep before its diocesan seminarians the prospect of their future incorporation into a particular diocese and its presbyterate. Seminarians should have opportunities and receive encouragement to learn about their diocesan structures and offices as well as to become acquainted with the priests who compose the presbyterate.

255. Pre-theology programs should include a program for pastoral formation that introduces seminarians, perhaps for the first time, to pastoral activity. Seminarians should be directed by qualified supervisors who are able to provide orientation to pastoral activity, basic skills development, and the beginnings of theological reflection.

256. College seminaries should provide a required program of apostolic activity, under the direction of a qualified director who has faculty status. Evaluation of college seminarians should include consideration of their performance in pastoral formation programs. They should be encouraged to understand the relationship of their apostolic activity to their personal, spiritual, and academic formation as well as their ongoing discernment of a priestly vocation.

257. In high school seminaries, opportunities for Christian service, both within and outside the seminary, should be provided according to a student's level of maturity in order to develop a capacity for generous self-giving.   Tithing

V. COMMUNITY

258. Priestly formation occurs in the context of a community whether as a seminary or a house of formation. It is "a continuation in the Church of the apostolic community gathered about Jesus" in which men called to share in a unique way in the priesthood of Christ relive today the formation offered to the Twelve by the Lord.[161] What follows also applies to religious seminarians *mutatis mutandis.*

259. The seminary's life in community mirrors ecclesial communion, which itself is rooted in the Blessed Trinity. This ecclesiology of communion lived out in seminary community is "decisive for understanding the identity of the priest, his essential dignity, and his vocation and mission among the People of God and in the world" (*Pastores dabo vobis*, no. 12). Viewed in this way, the seminary community is the essential formational matrix for those preparing for ordained ministry, which itself "has a radical communitarian form' and can only be carried out as a 'collective work'" (*Pastores dabo vobis*, no. 17). The seminary community, then, is committed

---

161 *Pastores dabo vobis*, nos. 60-61.

to fostering the human, spiritual, intellectual, and pastoral formation of future priests.[162]

260.   The essential work of the seminary takes place in the context of community. Personal growth and character development should progress together harmoniously within a deepening spiritual life. The seminary is a school of human virtue, of growth in honesty, integrity, intellectual rigor, hard work, and tolerance, where the common good is built with solidarity and discipline—all leavened by humor and healthy enjoyment. The seminary also must be a school of spiritual growth in which seminarians are formed into men of prayer, imbued with those virtues that only grace can bring: faith, hope, and charity. The seminary should help the seminarians develop the relationship and dialogue skills necessary for healthy interpersonal relationships as priests.

261.   Seminary programs of formation have two focal points: the seminary community and its public life as an environment for growth and development that includes many different kinds of relationships, *and* individual seminarians as they strive to interiorize the values of the spiritual life and integrate the lessons of human, spiritual, intellectual, and pastoral formation. The interplay between individual and community lies at the heart of formation.

262.   The experience of seminary community plays a significant role in the personal and spiritual growth of seminarians. Each level of seminary from high school through the theologate will shape community in a particular way. Still, at every level, community is formative in similar ways. The give-and-take between those who share the priesthood as a common vocation sets the right context for formation. Such interaction provides mutual support, promotes tolerance and fraternal correction, and gives an opportunity for the development of leadership and talent among seminarians. It also can motivate seminarians to develop a sense of self-sacrifice and a spirit of collaboration. Community also should provide the context in which those qualities necessary for ministerial leadership can be nurtured and demonstrated: "emotional maturity, personal faith, moral integrity, and social concern."[163] The seminarians and faculty form the heart of

---

162   See *Pastores dabo vobis*, no. 61.
163   ATS 4.2.1.1.

the seminary community, and this reality needs careful cultivation so that the distinctive aims of seminary formation can be achieved.

NORMS FOR COMMUNITY

263.   Seminarians are to be fully committed to the life of the seminary community and learn how to contribute generously to it and to receive humbly from its resources.

264.   With an eye toward the exercise of future pastoral responsibilities, seminarians should give evidence of an ability to follow a reasonable schedule with community prayer at its heart, allowing time for a healthy balance of personal prayer, study, enjoyment of the arts, physical exercise, leisure, and social interaction; seminarians should develop discerning habits in reading, the use of various media, the Internet, and entertainment in general.[164]

265.   Each seminary must have a handbook based on the *Program of Priestly Formation*, approved by the diocesan bishop or religious ordinary, in which the expectations of the formation program of the seminary are clearly stated. These expectations specify the human, spiritual, intellectual, and pastoral components of that formation program and include a rule of life. The handbook forms the basis of an annual evaluation of the seminarians and is regularly reviewed and updated. In addition to a rule of life, the handbook also includes the seminary's mission statement, policies and procedures, criteria for admission and ongoing evaluation, appropriate calendars and schedules, and a description of faculty roles and house jobs.

266.   A rule of life is necessary to regulate day-to-day living and to articulate the common values that give a community integrity and purpose. A rule of life addresses the essentials of community living while avoiding excessive detail that would stifle individual initiative or talent. The rule of life provides a clear statement of the behavioral expectations

---

164   See Congregation for Catholic Education, *Guide to the Training of Future Priests Concerning the Instruments of Social Communications* (1986); *Ratio fundamentalis*, no. 68.

of seminarians pursuing a priestly vocation. It also seeks to balance freedom, responsibility, accountability, activities, and solitude.

267.   The rector's conferences are especially helpful in aiding students to interpret rightly their life in common, their discernment of vocation to the priesthood, and the human and spiritual virtues they strive to appropriate.

268.   The expectations and procedures of the evaluation process should be detailed in the student handbook and explained clearly to the student body by the rector or his delegate each year.

269.   Matters pertaining to celibate and chaste living must be included in the seminary rule of life. This rule must also foster simplicity of life, encouraging fasting, almsgiving, and the asceticism demanded by a Christian life and the priestly state. The seminary environment itself should foster a simple way of life and a spirit of forthright detachment. Seminarians should be made aware that they are accountable for the proper stewardship of material goods and personal health. The rule of life must encourage appropriate respect for those in authority, and a mature sense of obedience.

270.   The seminary should create a climate for mutual respect, communication, and collaboration as a contribution to the overall development of the seminarians as they interact with many other individuals and communities as well. Men and women mingle with seminarians in a variety of settings: personal, academic, pastoral, and ecumenical. The interaction of seminarians with seminary administrative staff and service personnel often reveals attitudes toward others in general. Seminarians' ongoing contact with their own family and home community should continue to form a significant dimension of their life. Seminarians should participate in parish activities and volunteer for service on a regular basis.

271.   The seminary community and individual seminarians should appreciate the presence of a multicultural, multiethnic, and international community within the seminary. This environment provides a mutually enriching dimension to a seminary community and reflects the realities of pastoral life awaiting seminarians. This diversity should also help seminarians develop a quality of adaptability to varied pastoral settings in their future priestly ministry.

VI. THE CONTINUING EVALUATION OF SEMINARIANS

272.   The continuing evaluation of seminarians is linked to their formation as well as to the Church's responsibility to discern vocations to priesthood as a gift from God. Since formation, whether human, spiritual, intellectual, or pastoral, assumes that a seminarian will be growing both in God's grace and in his free, human response to that grace, it is important that there be a process to note the markers of that growth. In this way, the Church provides candidates for priestly ministry with encouragement to continue their formation and wisdom to identify ways in which that formation may take deeper root. The Church's responsibility to discern the authenticity of vocations also implies that there is some process whereby the Church, usually working through the seminary, scrutinizes the candidate's aptness and readiness to assume the responsibilities of ordained ministry. This ongoing evaluation of seminarians, then, fosters growth in formation while continuing the process of discernment.

NORMS FOR THE CONTINUING EVALUATION OF SEMINARIANS

273.   The seminary is responsible for the continuing evaluation of seminarians regarding their progress in priestly formation. The process of evaluation should be clearly described in detail in the student handbook. The seminary should have a written statement of the criteria used in evaluating seminarians. Such evaluation is primarily the responsibility of the rector and faculty. It should also involve the input of the seminarians themselves, their various supervisors, and their peers.

274.   Each seminary must provide a procedure for the evaluation of the seminarians. As part of this procedure, each seminary should ensure that as many faculty as possible are engaged in this process; that the seminarians are apprised of their progress as early as possible in their formation, particularly if there are concerns; that the formation advisor/mentor regularly communicates with the seminarian; that the seminarians have a procedure for responding to matters raised in the evaluation process; that confidentiality, as articulated by the seminary, is observed; and that all doubts are resolved in favor of the Church. The process of evaluation

should be conducted in an atmosphere of mutual trust and confidence. It should promote the continued growth of the seminarian in the four dimensions of formation.

275.   Seminarians are accountable for all aspects of priestly formation within the parameters of the external forum. This includes participation in spiritual exercises, the spiritual direction program, liturgical exercises, and community life as well as the academic and pastoral dimensions of priestly formation. This approach is taken because all the aspects of priestly formation are "intimately interwoven and should not be separated from one another."[165]

276.   A seminarian's self-evaluation can be a valuable instrument. Seminarians should prepare such evaluations with an honest and candid examination of themselves in the areas of human, spiritual, intellectual, and pastoral formation. They should recognize their strengths and weaknesses, and positive qualities as well as areas of needed growth. It is the responsibility of the seminarian to show positive qualities that recommend his advancement in formation. This self-evaluation is done best in consultation with a formation advisor/mentor.

277.   Peer evaluations are recommended as helpful in the evaluation process. Such evaluations should be conducted in a responsible and confidential manner. Seminarians completing peer evaluations should be exhorted to do so with honesty and in a spirit of charity. Positive or negative opinions concerning the suitability of a peer for advancement should be expressed clearly.

278.   The seminary should require an evaluation of a seminarian's summer activities from his appropriate supervisor. This report should also give attention to the areas of human, spiritual, intellectual, and pastoral formation.

279.   The evaluative process culminates in a yearly written report from the rector to the diocesan bishop or religious ordinary that provides a clear estimation of the seminarian's progress in the areas of human, spiritual, intellectual, and pastoral formation. The annual report should include the results of the faculty vote regarding the seminarian's advancement, sup-

---

165   ATS 4.1.1.

plying the number of affirmative and negative votes as well as the number of abstentions. Both negative votes and abstentions should be explained.

280.   The annual evaluation should include a well-founded judgment concerning the suitability of the seminarian for advancement to the next year of formation. The evaluation report should be detailed. The qualities listed in canon law as requirements for promotion to Orders should be considered at each stage of advancement: integral faith, right intention, requisite knowledge, good reputation, integral morals and proven virtues, and the requisite physical and psychological health.[166] The evaluation should provide a judgment of the seminarian's aptitude for priestly life and ministry as well as an estimation of his capacity to lead a chaste, celibate life. The stage or year in which the seminarian is currently in formation should be considered in assessing his readiness for advancement. The following issues in each area of formation are to be considered and are to be applied, according to the principle of gradualism, at each level of formation:

a. Human Formation:
— The human qualities of truthfulness, respect for others, justice, humility, integrity, affability, generosity, kindness, courtesy, integrity, and prudence
— The capacity to relate to others in a positive manner and the ability to get along with others and work with them in the community
— Good self-knowledge, self-discipline, and self-mastery, including emotional self-control
— Good physical and mental health
— A balanced lifestyle and balance in making judgments
— Affective maturity and healthy psychosexual development; clarity of male sexual identity; an ability to establish and maintain wholesome friendships; the capacity to maintain appropriate boundaries in relationships
— Skills for leadership and collaboration with women and men
— Capacity to receive and integrate constructive criticism

---

166   See CIC, c. 1029; CCEO, c. 758.

— Simplicity of life, stewardship of resources, and responsibility for financial obligations
— Mature respect for and cooperation with church authority
— Engagement in the community life of the seminary

b. Spiritual Formation: There should be accountability in the external forum for seminarians' participation in spiritual exercises of the seminary and their growth as men of faith. Within the parameters of the external forum, habits of prayer and personal piety are also areas of accountability.
— Commitment to a life of prayer and the ability to assist others in their spiritual growth
— Abiding love for the sacramental life of the Church, especially the Holy Eucharist and Penance
— A loving knowledge of the Word of God and prayerful familiarity with that Word
— Appreciation of and commitment to the Liturgy of the Hours
— Fidelity to the liturgical and spiritual program of the seminary, including the daily celebration of the Eucharist
— Fidelity to regular spiritual direction and regular celebration of the Sacrament of Penance and a habit of spiritual reading
— A positive embrace of a lifelong commitment to chaste celibacy, obedience, and simplicity of life
— A love for Jesus Christ and the Church, for the Blessed Virgin Mary and the saints
— A spirit of self-giving charity toward others

c. Intellectual Formation:
— Love for truth as discovered by faith and reason
— Fidelity to the Word of God and to the Magisterium
— Knowledge of Catholic doctrine and adherence to it
— Interest and diligence in seminary studies
— Successful completion of seminary academic requirements
— Ability to exercise the ministry of the Word: to proclaim, explain, and defend the faith
— Knowledge of languages that will be necessary or suitable for the exercise of their pastoral ministry

d. Pastoral Formation:
— A missionary spirit, zeal for evangelization, and ecumenical commitment
— A spirit of pastoral charity, a quest for justice, and an openness to serve all people
— A special love for and commitment to the sick and suffering, the poor and outcasts, prisoners, immigrants, and refugees
— Demonstration of appropriate pastoral and administrative skills and competencies for ministry
— Ability to exercise pastoral leadership
— Ability to carry out pastoral work collaboratively with others and an appreciation for the different charisms and vocations within the Church
— The ability to work in a multicultural setting with people of different ethnic, racial, and religious backgrounds
— A commitment to the proclamation, celebration, and service of the Gospel of life
— Energy and zeal for pastoral ministry

281.   The content of the annual evaluation should be communicated to each seminarian in a constructive way.

282.   The annual evaluation may be concurrent with the scrutiny required for each liturgical ritual that marks the seminarian's advancement toward the priesthood, providing clear indications regarding his suitability.[167] The norms of the Church are to be observed regarding admission to candidacy and institution into the ministries of lector and acolyte (Latin Church)[168] or minor orders (Eastern Churches).[169] The proper documentation must be collected for the scrutiny for each stage. The procedures and documentation required prior to ordination to the diaconate and to the priesthood are to be completed.[170]

283.   Seminarians should have exercised the ministries of lector and acolyte (Latin Church) or minor orders (Eastern Churches) for a suitable period of time before ordination to the diaconate (CIC, c. 1035§1).

---

167   See Circular Letter of the Congregation for Divine Worship and the Discipline of the Sacraments concerning *Scrutinies Regarding the Suitability of Candidates for Orders* (November 10, 1997).
168   See CIC, cc. 1034-1035; *motu proprio* of Pope Paul VI: *Ministeria quaedam* and *Ad pascendum*.
169   See CCEO, c. 758§1, 5°.
170   See CIC, cc. 1050-1052; CCEO, cc. 769-770.

There is to be an interval of at least six months between the conferral of the ministry of acolyte (Latin Church) or minor orders (Eastern Church) and ordination to the diaconate (CIC, c. 1035§2). Prior to ordination to the diaconate, the candidate is to make a canonical retreat (CIC, c. 1039; CCEO, c. 772), take the Oath of Fidelity,[171] and make the Profession of Faith (CIC, c. 833, 6°; CCEO, c. 187§2). The candidate is to be at least 23 years of age (CIC, c. 1031§1; CCEO, c. 759). He is to have completed at least five years of philosophy and theology (CIC, c. 1032§1; CCEO, c. 760), have received candidacy (except for vowed members of clerical institutes) (CIC, c. 1034), be able to articulate the theology and expectations of the diaconate (CIC, c. 1028), and petition his ordinary to be ordained expressing his free intention and permanent commitment (CIC, cc. 1034§1, 1036; CCEO, c. 761). The seminary is to certify to the ordinary that all these requirements have been met (CIC, c. 1050, 1°; CCEO, c. 769, 1°). The rector verifies that the candidate for the diaconate accepts the teachings of the Church, prays the complete Liturgy of the Hours, attends daily Mass, receives the Sacrament of Penance regularly, and is committed to a life of celibacy.

284.   A judgment concerning the suitability of a candidate to receive the diaconate as a transitional step to priesthood includes a judgment concerning his suitability for priestly ministry. It is not possible to admit a candidate to the diaconate in the face of doubts concerning his suitability for the priesthood. For this reason the judgment reached by the scrutiny undertaken with a view to ordination to the diaconate is decisive. If this judgment is positive, it could be changed in the course of the next scrutiny prior to priestly ordination only in the light of new and grave information.[172]

285.   Deacons should have exercised the diaconal order for a suitable period of time before being ordained to the priesthood (CIC, c. 1032§2). There is to be an interval of at least six months between a seminarian's ordination to the diaconate and his ordination to the priesthood (CIC, c. 1031§1). He is to be at least 25 years of age (CIC, c. 1031§1; CCEO, c. 759§1). He is to have completed six years of philosophy and theology (CIC, c. 1032§1; CCEO, c. 760§1) and be able to articulate the theology

---

171   See *Acta Apostolicae Sedis* (AAS) 81 (1989) 104-106.
172   See Circular Letter of the Congregation for Divine Worship and the Discipline of the Sacraments concerning *Scrutinies Regarding the Suitability of Candidates for Orders* (November 10, 1997), no. 11.

and expectations of the priesthood (CIC, c. 1028). He is to petition his diocesan bishop or religious ordinary to be ordained expressing his free intention and permanent commitment (CIC, c. 1036; CCEO, c. 761). The seminary is to certify to the ordinary that all these requirements have been met (CIC, c. 1050, 1°; CCEO, c. 769, 3°). The rector verifies the candidate for the priesthood is ready to assume the teaching, sanctifying, and governing mission of Christ. Furthermore, he should demonstrate pastoral love for others and faithful obedience, in conformity with Christ. Prior to ordination to the priesthood, the candidate is to make a canonical retreat (CIC, c. 1039; CCEO, c. 772) and take the Oath of Fidelity.[173]

286.   The final judgment about a seminarian's admission to candidacy, institution into the ministries of lector and acolyte, and ordination to the diaconate and priesthood belongs to the diocesan bishop or religious ordinary. He is to have positive evidence proving the suitability of a candidate for Orders (CIC, c. 1052§1; CCEO, c. 770). The seminary's evaluations are important in providing this evidence. If such positive evidence is lacking, the seminary must not recommend the advancement of a seminarian.

287.   Seminarians who lack the positive qualities for continuing in formation should not be advanced in the seminary program. They should be advised to leave the seminary. Seminarians not recommended for advancement should be notified as early as possible and in a constructive manner. In these cases, an opportunity should be provided for the seminarian to present his self-assessment; others who can speak on the seminarian's behalf should also be heard.

288.   When there is doubt about the readiness of a seminarian for advancement, consideration can be given to a recommendation of a period of probation outside the seminary. The time period involved should be specified, not open-ended. The period of probation should have clearly identified goals and means to assess the achievement of goals. Likewise, appropriate supervision is necessary so that this period away would help bring about needed growth for a possible return to the seminary. If doubts remain after this period, the seminarian should not continue in formation.

---

173   See Circular Letter of the Congregation for Divine Worship and the Discipline of the Sacraments concerning *Scrutinies Regarding the Suitability of Candidates for Orders* (November 10, 1997), Enclosure IV.

289.   Houses of formation should maintain appropriate collaborative relationships with the administration and faculty of union-model theologates and other study centers in order to aid the evaluation of their candidates.

Seminaries: Governance, Administration, and Faculty Governance

INTRODUCTION

290.   Seminaries are to be a continuation in the Church of the apostolic community gathered around Jesus.[174] This basic organizing principle means the seminary is first and foremost a learning community of the disciples of Jesus. At the same time, the seminary is a community of charity and friendship, where fraternal bonds are anchored in genuine relationships to the Lord and his Body, the Church. Finally, the seminary is a worshipping and praying community that finds its source and summit in the celebration of the Eucharist.

GOVERNANCE

291.   Governance is the responsibility of the diocesan bishop or religious ordinary. In order to fulfill this responsibility, the diocesan bishop or religious ordinary may work in collaboration with the seminary board or boards and others the bishop or religious ordinary may delegate. The governing authority establishes the mission and exercises general oversight of the seminary. The seminary should have a precise program "characterized by its being organized and unified, by its being in harmony or correspondence with one aim which justifies the existence of the seminary: preparation of future priests" (*Pastores dabo vobis*, no. 61).

292.   In their efforts to "organize and unify," diocesan bishops and religious ordinaries, for their respective seminaries, ensure that the directives of the Holy See and the United States Conference of Catholic Bishops are fully and effectively implemented through the mission, goals, and

---

174   See *Pastores dabo vobis*, no. 60.

programs of the seminary; through long-range planning; through the appointment of the rector; and through seminary policies. In keeping with the principle of subsidiarity, the governing authority does not normally enter directly into the day-to-day administration of the seminary, since such duties are the responsibility of the rector.[175]

THE ROLE OF THE DIOCESAN BISHOP OR RELIGIOUS ORDINARY

293.   The diocesan bishop or the religious ordinary oversees the implementation of the *Decree on the Training of Priests* and the *Program of Priestly Formation*, and he ensures that the seminary statutes correspond to canon law. The diocesan bishop or religious ordinary discharges these responsibilities personally and through the seminary board(s), the rector, seminary administration, faculty, and staff. He should visit the seminary and have vigilance for the seminarians. He should also encourage and support the rector, the administration, and the faculty in their dedication to this apostolate.[176]

294.   The diocesan bishop or religious ordinary ensures that the administration and faculty of the seminary offer a program in accord with the mind of the Church—including an approved written rule of life—and in keeping with the standards of the seminary's accrediting agency.

295.   It is essential that frequent and open communication be maintained between ecclesiastical authorities and the rector, the administration, and faculty to discuss the changing needs of the Church, the progress of seminarians, and developments in the seminary program.

296.   At times, candidates for the diocesan priesthood attend seminaries owned and operated by religious and not by a diocese. In such instances, the local diocesan bishop has canonical responsibility for the welfare of all diocesan seminarians in attendance there.[177] Accordingly, he should be in regular communication with the seminary administration and accorded a voice in the governance of the seminary.

---

175   See CIC, c. 260.
176   See CIC, c. 259§2; CCEO, cc. 336§1, 356§2.
177   See Bishops' Committee on Priestly Formation, "Relationship of the Local Ordinary (Bishop) to the Seminary Owned and Operated by Religious" (1981).

297.   The formation of religious candidates for priesthood is the responsibility of each institute or society and is regulated by the constitutions and other canonical legislation or directives pertaining to religious, as well as by the directives of this *Program of Priestly Formation.*

298.   Most religious seminaries are collaborative ventures of several religious institutes or societies. Responsibility for the canonical form of governance belongs to those who hold ecclesiastical jurisdiction. The statutes of such institutions must be approved by the competent ecclesiastical authority. The Holy See must approve priestly formation centers formed by a number of religious institutes or societies.

SEMINARY BOARDS

299.   A variety of structures is legitimately used in the governance of seminaries in the United States. In situations with multiple boards, the bylaws of each should establish the clear jurisdiction and purpose of each board or corporation. Care should be taken to guarantee that the bylaws of these corporations and boards are canonically proper and in accord with civil law, providing for suitable ecclesiastical oversight.

300.   An advisory board can provide a valuable service to the seminary by offering wise counsel to the diocesan bishop or religious ordinary on governance of the seminary in accord with church law, the *Program of Priestly Formation*, and the standards of the seminary's accrediting agency.

301.   Members of the board should represent the clergy, religious, and laity who share a concern for priestly formation and higher education. They should be selected from the local churches and religious institutes or societies that the seminary serves. The board ought to reflect the multicultural composition of the Church in the region or diocese(s) it serves.

302.   Boards should have a well-articulated policy and an active practice of board development, so that board members can fulfill their responsibilities more effectively. This policy should include a provision for the regular evaluation of the board's own performance.

303.   When seminary boards have fiduciary responsibility for the seminary, the members should be well prepared for that role and discharge their responsibility effectively.

FORMATION OF GOVERNANCE POLICY[178]

304.   The process used to form governance policy should be clearly defined by the bishop or religious ordinary in consultation with the seminary board(s) and the rector. The process should clearly identify the scope of governance authority and responsibility, while protecting the principle of subsidiarity and avoiding intrusion into administrative matters of the seminary.

305.   The most important governance policy is the mission statement of the seminary. Each mission statement must incorporate a clear understanding of and commitment to the formation of men for the ministerial priesthood. It is also important for the seminary to respond to the priorities of local churches and communities it services through the establishment of appropriate policies.

306.   Proposals regarding governance policy are often initiated at the level of the seminary community where concrete needs and problems occur. After review by the seminary faculty and administration, policy proposals of major importance are presented by the rector to the seminary board and appropriate ecclesiastical authority for approval. Consultation of the seminary community, including seminarians themselves, should be characteristic of policy making in seminaries.

PLANNING

307.   Planning provides for the long-range stability of the seminary, the effective implementation of its mission, and good stewardship of all associated resources. A realistic conception of the seminary's future should include effective planning regarding personnel, facilities, enrollment, finances, budget, and development. In their efforts to plan for the seminary's future, bishops and religious ordinaries should enlist the assistance of the seminary board as well as the rector, the administration, and the faculty of the seminary.

---

178   By "governance policy" in this document is meant those norms, laws, and decrees that strictly speaking flow from the rights and obligations inherent in the authority of the diocesan bishop or religious ordinary. Administrative policies are the responsibility of those deputed for the internal operation of the seminary, particularly the rector. Administrative policy means operational rules, regulations, and procedures that implement the mission and governance policy approved by the diocesan bishop or religious ordinary.

308. The Scriptures impose on ecclesiastical authorities the obligation of finding worthy and faithful co-workers in the service of God's people.[179] Diocesan bishops and religious ordinaries should encourage exemplary priests to enter the seminary apostolate and be willing to release them for such service. Seminaries should cooperate with diocesan bishops and religious ordinaries in the preparation of priest personnel. Deacons, religious, and lay men and women should also be encouraged to prepare for work in seminary education and receive assistance when appropriate. Dioceses and seminaries must honestly plan for the financial commitment that this requires.

309. Facilities should be adequate to the seminary's needs and suitable for an institution of either secondary or higher education. The seminary buildings should provide an atmosphere conducive to human, spiritual, intellectual, and pastoral formation.

310. Effective education requires other physical resources, such as libraries, laboratories, computer facilities, and other information technology centers.

311. Adequate enrollment is a critical component of a healthy priestly formation program. Consistently low enrollment may endanger the effectiveness of community life and learning. It will normally result in poor stewardship of resources and may affect the morale of the seminary community. Careful monitoring of the enrollment of qualified students is critical for realistic planning. In those seminaries where enrollment has been consistently low for a protracted period, consolidation should be investigated.

312. A seminary must have sufficient financial resources to achieve its mission effectively now and in the future. The raising of annual operating income as well as endowments[180] should be planned and developed in such a way as to allow the rector to fulfill his essential role as pastor of the seminary community.[181]

---

179   See 1 Tm 5:12; see *Pastores dabo vobis*, no. 65.
180   See CIC, c. 264; CCEO, c. 341.
181   See CIC, c. 262; CCEO, c. 336§2.

Administration

STRUCTURE

313.   The administrative structure of the seminary will depend on the nature, size, model, and level of the priestly formation program. It is important that administrative structures and the responsibilities of administrative personnel be clearly defined in light of the purpose of the seminary. Descriptions given here should be adapted to each program.

ADMINISTRATION

314.   Administrators in seminaries should be conscious that they are forming seminarians by the very work of administration, as they model for them this pastoral activity. The exercise of authority should be clearly seen as service.

Administration is always relational:

- It values the life and potential of each member of the community.
- It nurtures and challenges growth in members of the community in accord with the Gospel and the tradition of the Church.
- It models mature Christian behavior.
- It values interior responsibility over simple external conformity.
- It enables others to be of service to the community.
- It respects and values the dignity of others.
- It is always to be a ministry of love.
- It promotes communication within the institution and between the institution and its constituencies.
- It operates by the principle of subsidiarity.

315.   Administrative policies should be made by the appropriate authorities in an atmosphere of trust and understanding. While adhering to the goals of priestly formation, administrators, faculty, and staff should respond appropriately to the needs and suggestions of seminarians. They should foster initiative as well as individual and group responsibility by observing the principles of subsidiarity and collaboration, while demon-

strating forthright and confident leadership. Seminary administrators have a unique opportunity to serve as models of leadership for seminarians.

ADMINISTRATIVE POSITIONS

316.   Seminaries may use different titles to describe necessary administrative functions. Whatever the determination of titles, the functions described below are needed for an effective priestly formation program. In keeping with the unique nature and purpose of the seminary, major administrative posts are normally assigned to priests. All administrative personnel should have adequate preparation and the experience necessary to carry out the responsibilities they are assigned. They should understand the mission of the Church and seminary and be supportive of it.

317.   Seminary administrators bear a special responsibility for planning, organizing, directing, and evaluating the implementation of the *Program of Priestly Formation* in their respective institutions.

The Rector

318.   The rector, always a priest, serves as the pastor of the seminary community.[182] He sets the direction and tone of the seminary program. By creating a climate of mutual confidence and trust, he elicits the full cooperation and involvement of faculty and students. His job description should be carefully drawn to ensure that he has the authority to discharge properly the responsibilities of his office. Given the extent and gravity of these responsibilities, the diocesan bishop or religious ordinary should ensure that the rector not have additional obligations outside the seminary that detract from his primary duties.

319.   The rector is appointed by appropriate ecclesiastical authority, who, according to local statutes, seeks consultation with the seminary board and other interested parties, including the faculty. He is to make a profession of faith and take the oath of fidelity at the beginning of his term.[183] The rector is responsible to the diocesan bishop or religious ordinary and should consult with him in matters of major concern. As a

---

182   See CIC, c. 262; CCEO, cc. 336§2, 341.
183   See CIC, c. 833, 6°.

rule the rector is also responsible to a seminary board, if a legal corporation exists. If the board is advisory, he should give thoughtful consideration to its counsel and take advantage of its expertise in administering the seminary.

320.   The rector serves as chief administrative officer and principal agent responsible for the implementation of the seminary program.[184] He should also maintain close contact with the bishops and religious ordinaries of the dioceses and religious institutes or societies that the seminary serves. In addition, he is often responsible for public relations and development, though he may delegate these tasks to others. Although these duties may call him away from the seminary, it is important that the rector serve as leader of the internal life of the seminary both as pastor and priestly model.

321.   The spiritual and personal welfare of faculty and students is a central responsibility of the rector. Regularly, the rector should give conferences to the seminary community. He should frequently preside at prayer and at the Eucharist.

322.   As provided for other members of the faculty, the rector should "be carefully prepared in sound doctrine, suitable pastoral experience and special spiritual and pedagogical training."[185] The rector should be a model of priestly virtue, able to live himself the qualities he encourages in students. A man of sound and prudent judgment, the rector should give evidence to a love of and dedication to the Church's service.

323.   Depending on the size and structure of the seminary, the rector may also assume some of the responsibilities of other administrators mentioned in this chapter, with the exception of the spiritual direction of seminarians.

Vice-Rector

324.   The vice-rector, always a priest, assists the rector in areas determined by the rector and each seminary's administrative structure. Tasks vary according to the needs of the particular seminary.

---

184   See CIC, c. 261; CCEO, c. 338§2.
185   *Optatam totius*, no. 5.

Director of Human Formation

325. The director of human formation is a priest who coordinates the human formation program of the seminary (see *Pastores dabo vobis*, nos. 43-44) in collaboration with the rector, other formation mentors/advisors, and seminary faculty and staff. The director and the formation faculty work in the external forum as agents of the rector. The director of human formation may also oversee the discipline of the seminary and the implementation of the Rule of Life. He should be exemplary for his personal maturity, pastoral experience, and appreciation of the psychological and human sciences.

326. The director oversees the annual evaluation process in collaboration with the rector, other formation mentors/advisors, and the seminary faculty and staff. The evaluation of seminarians can benefit from a team or faculty group assisting in the process.

327. The director of human formation makes provision for psychological and counseling services in areas distinct from spiritual direction. These services are made available to seminarians for their personal and emotional development as candidates for the priesthood. The counseling given should be consistent with the policy and practice of the total seminary program. The director should ensure that those employed as counselors for seminarians are well versed in and supportive of the Church's expectations of candidates for the priesthood.

Formation Mentors/Advisors

328. Formation mentors/advisors monitor seminarians assigned to them in all four areas of formation and they assist in the evaluation process. They should be priests who are exemplary in their dedication to the Church and to the ministerial priesthood. They should be mature and faithful Catholics who possess a background in human development, Catholic spirituality, and related areas. These formation mentors/advisors function exclusively in the external forum and are not to engage in matters that are reserved for the internal forum and the spiritual director.

Director of Spiritual Formation

329.   This priest is appointed by the diocesan bishop or religious ordinary and assists the rector by coordinating the entire spiritual formation program, giving it unity and direction.

330.   The director of spiritual formation makes provision for the individual spiritual direction of all seminarians. He meets regularly with the spiritual directors, providing supervision and assistance for their work.

331.   Either the director of spiritual formation or the director of liturgy provides for the liturgical life and prayer of the seminary community, making provision for the daily celebration of the Eucharist, the Liturgy of the Hours, and opportunities for celebration of the Sacrament of Penance. He is also responsible for retreats and days of recollection, making sure they are well planned and carefully executed.

Spiritual Directors

332.   Priests who are assigned as spiritual directors and designated for this function by the diocesan bishop or religious ordinary[186] are responsible for the individual spiritual direction of seminarians. Those who act in this capacity should be exemplary priests who are dedicated to the Church's service and to the ministerial priesthood. They should be wise, seasoned priests and possess some formal training in spirituality and related areas of expertise. Individual spiritual directors should continue to develop their skills and abilities through ongoing education programs and through in-service discussions with their fellow directors, taking care to preserve confidentiality in matters of the internal forum.

333.   Since spiritual direction takes place in the internal forum, the relationship of seminarians to their spiritual director is a privileged and confidential one. Spiritual directors may not participate in the evaluation of those they currently direct or whom they directed in the past.[187]

---

186   See CIC, c. 239§2; CCEO, c. 339§1.
187   See CIC, c. 240§2; CCEO, c. 339§3.

Academic Dean/Director of Intellectual Formation

334.   The director of intellectual formation, normally a priest, is the academic dean, who normally should possess a terminal degree and assists the rector in intellectual formation, including faculty hiring and development. The academic dean administers the intellectual formation program of the seminary in all its aspects: curriculum, courses, methods of instruction, and the academic quality and performance of faculty and students.

335.   In the case of collaborative seminaries, this director coordinates the academic work of the seminarians at the affiliated college or university.

336.   The director of intellectual formation may be assisted by a registrar, who is responsible for maintaining the academic records of students.

Director of Pastoral Formation

337.   The director of pastoral formation assists the rector in the pastoral formation of seminarians. The director coordinates the pastoral activities of students, so that they engage effectively in pastoral programs, reflect on their work, and gain deeper insight into the mission of the Church.

338.   The director provides an evaluation of the seminarians' work, calling attention to their strengths and their potential for general and specialized ministries.

339.   The director provides adequate pastoral supervision for the seminarians, including the orientation and training of adjunct field-education supervisors who work directly with the seminarians in their pastoral assignments.

340.   If the director of pastoral formation is more than an organizer of field education experiences, then this position should be filled by a priest.

Librarian

341.   The librarian ordinarily enjoys faculty status and administers the library according to the standards of the respective professional accrediting and educational associations. The librarian ordinarily reports to the academic dean.

Development and Public Relations Officer

342.   A person may be appointed to assist the rector in planning, communications, public relations, and fund raising. This officer makes the seminary known to the general public, especially priests, vocation directors, schools, parishioners, and others, in an effort to attract new seminarians and gain support for the seminary.

Business Manager

343.   The business manager or treasurer assists the rector in the stewardship of the financial and physical resources of the seminary.[188] The business manager assists the rector in budget preparation and implementation as well as supervision of service personnel.

FACULTY

Conditions of Service

344.   The central role of the seminary faculty is highlighted in the documents of the Church. The qualities necessary for faculty members have been stated generically by the Second Vatican Council: pastoral experience and spiritual, academic, and professional preparation.[189]

345.   All members of the academic and formational faculty of the seminary are approved and appointed by the competent ecclesiastical authority on recommendation of the rector according to the approved statutes of the institution.[190] In order to teach on an ecclesiastical faculty, a canonical mission from the appropriate ecclesiastical authority is required.[191] In both cases, such commissioning represents a collaborative link between the faculty member and the Magisterium. "The theologian's code of conduct, which obviously has its origin in the service of the Word of God, is here

---

188   See CIC, c. 239§1; CCEO, cc. 338§1, 339§1.
189   See *Optatam totius*, no. 5; CIC, c. 253§1; CCEO, cc. 340§1, 351.
190   See *Optatam totius*, no. 5; CIC, c. 253§1; CCEO, cc. 340§1, 351.
191   See John Paul II, *Sapientia christiana* (*On Ecclesiastical Universities and Faculties*), no. 27, 1; CIC, c. 818; CCEO, c. 644.

reinforced by the commitment the theologian assumes in accepting his office, making the profession of faith, and taking the oath of fidelity."[192]

346.   The professors should have advanced, preferably terminal, degrees in their teaching areas. Professors in the sacred sciences, as well as philosophy, should possess a doctorate or licentiate from a university or institution recognized by the Holy See.[193] Priest faculty members should have appropriate experience in pastoral ministry.

347.   As a general rule, professors for significant portions of the course of studies in the major theological disciplines ought to be priests.[194] To provide excellent and competent faculty, diocesan bishops and religious ordinaries should be generous in encouraging priests to prepare for seminary work or in releasing their priests for this ministry, even if the seminary is not their own.

348.   Priests who are responsible for the human, spiritual, intellectual, and pastoral dimensions of priestly formation can be assisted by outstanding laypersons and/or non-ordained religious, all of whom have a particular expertise that can contribute to priestly formation.[195]

349.   Seminaries should establish long-range plans for faculty development. This should include plans for recruiting and supporting faculty, as well as plans for faculty to improve their teaching skills and scholarship.

350.   The nature of high school and college seminary formation and the breadth of expertise required for a liberal arts education mean that the dedicated presence of many lay men and women will play an especially important role on these levels. By modeling a love for the Church as she is, a wholehearted fidelity to her teaching, a loyalty to the pope and bishops, an appreciation of the priesthood, and a collaborative spirit in ministry, men and women religious and lay men and women make an important contribution to priestly formation on all levels.

---

192   Congregation for the Doctrine of the Faith, Instruction on the Ecclesial Vocation of the Theologian (1990), no. 22, http://www.vatican.va/roman_curia/congregations/cfaith/documents/rc_con_cfaith_doc_19900524_theologian-vocation_en.html. See CIC, c. 833§7°; CCEO, c. 187§2; Congregation for the Doctrine of the Faith, Professio fidei et iusiurandum fidelitatis (Formula to be used for the profession of faith and for the oath of fidelity to assume an office to be exercised in the name of the Church), AAS 81 (1989) 104ff.

193   See CIC, c. 253§1; CCEO, cc. 340§1, 351.

194   See Ratio fundamentalis, no. 33.

195   See Pastores dabo vobis, no. 66.

351.   All faculty members should be dedicated to the total formation of the students, willing to form with them a genuine educational community.[196] Faculty teach first by the quality of their lives. Faculty members—priests, religious, and laity—alike must therefore witness to the Gospel in their own lives.

352.   Every faculty member influences seminarians' growth in priestly maturity. Love for the Eucharist as a source and sign of unity within the seminary program must be clearly evident in the life and attitude of each member of the faculty. Therefore, regular participation in seminary liturgies is encouraged.

353.   Some of the seminary faculty share responsibility in all areas of the priestly formation program, including the spiritual and the pastoral formation of candidates. Full-time priest faculty, who also serve as spiritual directors and formation mentors/advisors, as a rule, should reside in the seminary (insofar as this is possible).

354.   It is important to recruit well-trained and experienced faculty from diverse ethnic, racial, and cultural backgrounds. This is especially important in those sections of the United States in which the Church and seminary student body reflect such diversity.

355.   If the seminary has a multicultural student body, the faculty should be encouraged to participate in programs and workshops that acquaint them with the specific situation and formational needs of their seminarians.

356.   In order to inculcate in seminarians sensitivity for issues of social justice, the seminary faculty first must possess an awareness of the significance of questions of peace, justice, and respect for life.

357.   Because of the importance of a pastoral orientation in seminary programs, some involvement by faculty in parish ministry or in other apostolic activities complements their work in the seminary. Likewise, seminary faculty are often called upon to help with diocesan projects and responsibilities. In this way, the seminary faculty contribute to the local

---

196   See *Pastores dabo vobis*, no. 66.

church or religious institute or society they serve. However, the demands of the seminary are to be given priority.

Faculty Organization

358.   A unity and harmony of effort should be present among all members of the faculty. In order to achieve this state, faculty handbooks should outline and clearly describe faculty expectations and responsibilities, rights, benefits, review, and grievance procedures.

359.   In order to maintain a qualified faculty in accordance with ecclesiastical and professional standards, there should be a faculty review process that regularly evaluates performance and offers direction for professional development. Review processes should consider the professor's teaching skills, academic competence, scholarly development (including publications), participation in professional societies, manner of life, personal dedication to the goals of priestly formation, and commitment to the Church.

360.   Seminaries are expected to hold regularly scheduled meetings of the full faculty. Both standing and ad hoc committees should regularly present appropriate and pertinent reports to the full faculty. The administration and faculty should periodically discuss the seminary's mission to educate men for the ministerial priesthood in light of the Church's doctrinal understanding of the presbyteral office.

361.   Together, members of the faculty should engage in a continuing evaluation of the programs of the seminary. This evaluation should consider the changing needs of the students, the church in which they will serve, and the norms of higher education. In order to accomplish this continual renewal, the faculty needs to be in regular communication with academic and ecclesial groups outside the seminary.

362.   The seminary should provide time and financial support for seminary professors to maintain professional competence in their fields of specialization through participation in professional associations, study leaves, and sabbaticals.

363.   An appropriate staff of secretaries should be provided for the faculty and the administration in order to free them for the more essential

tasks of their assigned offices and for personal renewal, serious scholarship, and student direction.

Doctrinal Responsibility

364.   Faculty members should have a firm foundation in the teaching of the Church. A fundamental task of the faculty is to present Catholic doctrine as formulated by the authoritative teaching office of the Church.[197]

365.   The freedom of expression required by the exigencies of theological science should be respected as well as the ability to do the research required for its progress.[198] Seminary statutes should provide for appropriate freedom of inquiry that allows and encourages study and reflection in teaching and publishing. This freedom must be understood in the context of the purpose of the seminary and balanced by the rights of the students, the institution, and the Church. "The freedom proper to theological research is exercised within the Church's faith. . . . In theology this freedom of inquiry is the hallmark of a rational discipline whose object is given by revelation, handed on and interpreted in the Church under the authority of the Magisterium, and received by faith."[199]

366.   Members of the faculty should be mindful of the varying degrees of theological certainty and should carefully distinguish between their own insights and other theological developments or opinions on the one hand and Catholic doctrine on the other.

367.   Faculty handbooks should contain clear procedures for the resolution of conflicts regarding the correctness of theological expression on the part of faculty members in accord with existing ecclesiastical norms.[200]

---

197   See *Pastores dabo vobis*, no. 67.
198   See CIC, c. 218; CCEO, c. 21.
199   *Instruction on the Ecclesial Vocation of the Theologian*, nos. 11-12.
200   See United States Conference of Catholic Bishops, *Doctrinal Responsibilities: Approaches to Promoting Cooperation and Resolving Misunderstandings Between Bishops and Theologians* (1989); *Pastores dabo vobis*, no. 67.

The Ongoing Formation of Priests

368.   The seminary program of priestly formation can appropriately be viewed as an initiation to sacramental life, not unlike the process envisioned in the Rite of Christian Initiation for Adults. Sacramental preparation and initiation necessarily includes a period of post-sacramental catechesis or mystagogia. Once celebrated, the sacraments are meant to be lived out, to be integrated into all dimensions of one's life, and to be a source of continuing transformation. For those who prepare for priestly ordination and for those who serve the formational process, this pattern of sacramental initiation implies the analogous necessity of helping seminarians commit themselves wholeheartedly to ongoing formation after ordination. The process and the journey of the ongoing formation of priests is both necessary and lifelong. Its purpose is not only the spiritual growth of the priest himself but also the continued effectiveness of his mission and ministry.

369.   The basic principle of ongoing formation for priests is contained in *Pastores dabo vobis*, no. 70: "one can speak of a *vocation 'within' the priesthood*. The fact is that God continues to call and send forth, revealing his saving plan in the historical development of the priest's life and the life of the Church and of society. It is in this perspective that the meaning of ongoing formation emerges. Permanent formation is necessary in order to discern and follow this constant call or will of God."

370.   The theologate ought to lay the foundations for the ongoing formation of priests across a lifetime of ministry. This is done in several ways:

- The seminary formation program must be imbued with a vision of life after ordination. "It is particularly important to be aware of and to respect the intrinsic *link between formation before ordination to the Priesthood and formation after ordination*" (*Pastores dabo vobis*, no. 70).

- The planning for ongoing formation and learning how to plan begins in the seminary. "Long-term preparation for ongoing formation should take place in the Major Seminary, where encouragement needs to be given to future priests to look forward to it, seeing its necessity, its advantages and the spirit in which it should be undertaken, and appropriate conditions for its realization need to be ensured" (*Pastores dabo vobis*, no. 70).

- The seminary must communicate its consciousness that it is incapable of providing everything needed for the life of priestly ministry. This conviction imparted to the students and to dioceses alike will encourage them to engage in the process of ongoing formation in all its dimensions—human, spiritual, intellectual, and pastoral.

- The seminary administration must be vigilant that programs lead to future habits of study, prayer, and formational involvement.

- On occasion, the seminary may be able to provide personnel and resources for transition programs into priesthood. Or it may invite newly and recently ordained back to reflect on their experience of transition and to engage in mystagogical catechesis that focuses on the rite of ordination and subsequent experiences of ministry.

371.   In the United States, the seminary—in its various formational efforts—ought to lead candidates for priesthood to the vision and practice of ongoing formation contained in the United States Conference of Catholic Bishops' document *The Basic Plan for the Ongoing Formation of Priests* (2001), which is the standard for those who are ordained priests. The chapter dealing with the newly ordained is an especially important marker for the formational journey of priests as they begin their ministry.

372.   A newly ordained priest who begins his first pastoral assignment and the process of ongoing formation should expect to find the following elements:

- Formal and informal welcoming by the diocesan bishop and presbyterate
- A first pastor who is sensitive to the needs of the newly ordained and able and willing to offer advice and direction
- A spiritual director

- Some group interaction with peers to reflect on the process of transition and the development of priestly identity and sources of support
- A mentor, as considered appropriate or necessary, with whom the newly ordained can reflect on ministry and life as a priest

373.   In the process of beginning priestly ministry and life, significant formational roles are played by the diocesan bishop, the director of ongoing formation for priests, and the entire presbyterate.

Conclusion

374.   The Catholic Church in the United States is deeply grateful to those dedicated to the noble enterprise of priestly preparation, mindful of its cherished heritage of seminary life. Likewise, the bishops of the Church in the United States are confident that this essential task will continue in a more effective way in the opening years of the third Christian millennium and are firmly committed to this mission. It is their hope that this fifth edition of the *Program of Priestly Formation* will serve this goal. Christ the Good Shepherd still calls men to follow him, to "cast out into the deep" (Lk 5:4), and to respond to his invitation to become a priest after his own heart, eager to be transformed through human, spiritual, intellectual, and pastoral formation.

375.   May the Lord who has begun this good work among us now bring it to completion.

ADDENDUM A.

Norms Concerning Applications for Priestly Formation from Those Previously Enrolled in a Formation Program

he National Conference of Catholic Bishops, in response to a special mandate from the Holy See (in relation to canon 455§1) contained in the *Instruction to the Episcopal Conferences* of the Congregation for Catholic Education of 8 March 1996 (Prot. N. 157/96) provides the following norms to assist the bishops of the United States, as well as those charged with the care of seminaries and houses of formation excepting those of Institutes of Consecrated Life and Societies of Apostolic Life, in their attention to the prescription of canon 241§3. The National Conference of Catholic Bishops therefore decrees that these norms are to be followed in reviewing an application for enrollment in a program of priestly formation submitted by one who has previously been enrolled in such a program or who has belonged to an institute of consecrated life or a society of apostolic life.

PREAMBLE

Pastores dabo vobis offers the theological framework for the Norms which follow:

> What is true of every vocation, is true specifically of the priestly vocation: the latter is a call, by the Sacrament of Holy Orders received in the Church, to place oneself at the service of the People of God with a particular belonging and configuration to

Jesus Christ and with the authority of acting "in the name and in the person" of him who is Head and Shepherd of the Church.

From this point of view, we understand the statement of the Synod Fathers: "The vocation of each priest exists in the Church and for the Church: through her this vocation is brought to fulfillment. Hence we can say that every priest receives his vocation from our Lord through the Church as a gracious gift, a grace *gratis data* (*charisma*). It is the task of the Bishop or the competent superior not only to examine the suitability and the vocation of the candidate but also to recognize it. This ecclesiastical element is inherent in a vocation to the priestly ministry as such. The candidate to the priesthood should receive his vocation not by imposing his own personal conditions, but accepting also the norms and conditions which the Church herself lays down, in the fulfillment of her responsibility." (*Pastores dabo vobis*, no. 35, citing *Propositio 5*)

PURPOSE

A primary responsibility of a diocesan bishop is the selection and training of candidates for the priesthood. This is likewise true for those major superiors responsible not only for the religious formation of candidates, but also for the priestly formation of at least some members. In the recent past, difficulties have arisen in this area, specifically regarding applicants who previously have been enrolled in a program of priestly formation or who have belonged to an institute of consecrated life or a society of apostolic life. Decisions regarding the suitability of individual applicants require both adequate information and a reasonable procedure to follow. These procedural norms have been formulated in an effort to serve diocesan bishops in fulfilling this weighty responsibility. These norms have been written out of a respect for the inherent rights and responsibilities of bishops, for the canonical norms which are already in place, and with respect for the juridical limitations of the episcopal conference. It is our hope that the following norms will promote mutual collaboration among bishops, major superiors, seminaries and priestly formation programs out of concern for the common good. More specifically, the purpose of this document is three fold:

1. To provide a process for full disclosure of all relevant information about a candidate who had previously been in formation and who subsequently applies for enrollment in a program of priestly formation

2. To facilitate a complete and confidential exchange of information about the applicant's prior enrollment in a program of priestly formation or his belonging to an institute of consecrated life or a society of apostolic life

3. To establish a process wherein former bishops and major superiors of an applicant can participate in a consultative review in regard to his application

NORMS FOR EVALUATION OF APPLICATIONS IN THESE CASES

1. At the time of departure from a seminary or diocesan formation program the diocesan bishop or seminary rector must inform the student by means of a written summary statement or letter of understanding that if he applies to a program of priestly formation in the future, relevant information will be communicated to the diocesan bishop, major superior, and, if necessary, the seminary rector, who is responsible for admission.

2. If an applicant has been dismissed from a program of priestly formation or from an institute of consecrated life or a society of apostolic life, no subsequent application will be considered in the two years following such dismissal. If the departure was other than a dismissal, sufficient time should be allotted to evaluate carefully his application and background.

Commentary
This waiting period is intended both to assist the applicant by giving him sufficient time to deal with the issues that led to his departure and to safeguard the diocese or religious community against the unnecessary risks of a speedy readmission. Reconsideration of a decision to dismiss should rarely, if ever,

be undertaken, and only if demonstrably clear and positive reasons to the contrary can be established.

The applicant is to be encouraged to seek the assistance and guidance of a spiritual director during this period. Spiritual directors and confessors are urged to avail themselves of this opportunity to remind these men of the particular requisites for admission to the seminary and eventual advancement to orders, and of the special challenges and difficulties of the priestly life, especially of the need for a firm commitment to the celibate state. However, the reserved nature of the internal forum would preclude those officials making admissions decisions from inquiring of the confessors or spiritual directors regarding these matters.

3. Diocesan and seminary application forms must include a question which specifically asks whether an applicant has ever applied to, been accepted or rejected by, or been dismissed from a diocesan formation program, seminary, institute of consecrated life or society of apostolic life.

4. At the time of future application the applicant must permit the release of all relevant information concerning his departure from any previous program of priestly formation or institute of consecrated life or society of apostolic life to the diocesan bishop, and, if necessary, the seminary rector, to whom he is applying. This release that the applicant signs must clearly state that he:

   a. consents to the sharing of all relevant information from previous formation programs with the diocesan bishop or rector to whom he is applying, and
   b. understands that no person has a right to be accepted into a program of priestly formation.

An applicant's refusal to provide the release of all relevant information provides sufficient grounds to reject the application. Likewise, inaccurate, incomplete, or misleading information provided by the applicant also provides sufficient grounds for rejection of the application.

It may be expected that the diocesan bishop will share the information with the seminary rector and/or other seminary admissions personnel. All persons who receive and/or review this information are reminded of the confidentiality required in these matters, and of the applicant's right to privacy and to a good reputation (see CIC, c. 220). The applicant should be advised of the information thus communicated which influences the admissions process.

Commentary

Accurate information on the previous departure from a seminary formation program or from an institute of consecrated life or a society of apostolic life is essential in evaluating a decision for subsequent admission to a seminary. Diocesan formation programs and other seminaries are encouraged to complete a final "exit" evaluation for departing students in order to have information on record regarding students at the time of leaving. This information (positive and/or negative) could be most helpful at a time of subsequent application.

5. Once the release has been executed and received, all seminaries attended and dioceses and/or institutes of consecrated life and societies of apostolic life with which the applicant was affiliated must be contacted in written form and should, if possible, be contacted through an oral, confidential interview with those persons responsible for the applicant's formation at that time. Those contacted should provide the pertinent information in a timely manner so as not to delay the process. For the sake of an accurate account of the interview, written notes should be taken and included in the applicant's confidential, permanent file. A record of calls or inquiries received by a diocese or seminary regarding a former student should be maintained. If any such institution or person responsible is not contacted with respect to a given application but nevertheless learns of it, all relevant information should be disclosed to the proper ecclesiastical authority.

Commentary

The authority handling the application is seriously obligated to fulfill this responsibility. "Those persons responsible" who should be contacted would include the major superior(s), bishop(s), vocation director(s), and rector(s) and/or dean(s) in office at the time the applicant was in formation. Action neither can nor should be taken regarding the application without this necessary information. The serious nature of this responsibility is outlined in the Circular Letter from the Congregation for Divine Worship and the Discipline of the Sacraments entitled, "Scrutinies regarding the Suitability of Candidates for Orders" (Prot. N. 589/97; see paragraph no. 8 and the introductory letter from the Pro-Prefect).

6. The diocesan bishop who decides to accept an applicant who was previously enrolled in a program of priestly formation or who belonged to an institute of consecrated life or a society of apostolic life must write a formal letter to the seminary or religious formation program where he is sending the applicant, with a copy to the bishop(s) of any diocese for which the applicant was previously in formation, or the major superior(s) of any institutes of consecrated life or society of apostolic life to which the candidate belonged. The letter should clearly state that:

   a. the applicant has been evaluated according to the norms outlined above;
   b. a thorough investigation of the applicant's background has been undertaken, including conversations with officials from the prior formation program in which he was enrolled including the current diocesan bishop(s) and major superior(s); and,
   c. it is his prudential judgment that the applicant is fit for seminary studies.

   A seminary or other priestly formation program may not accept a student if such a formal letter has not been submitted by the diocesan bishop or major superior who recommends the applicant. It is understood that seminaries retain the authority not to accept students judged by their admission procedures to be unsuitable, even when such a formal letter has been received.

7. If, after the evaluation of the application has been completed, the applicant is not accepted, it may be helpful for the proper authority to disclose to him the basic reasons why he was not accepted into the seminary or formation program.

8. In the case where the diocesan bishop has reservations about the judgment for a particular applicant, he may seek advice from the Committee on Priestly Formation.

Commentary

In formulating his judgment, the bishop is assisted by the direction given in the *Code of Canon Law*, canon 241. Section one of that canon states that the diocesan bishop is to admit to the major seminary only those candidates whose human, moral, spiritual and intellectual gifts, as well as physical and psychological health and right intention show the applicant's capability to dedicate himself permanently to the sacred ministries. Section three of the same canon addresses the cases at hand, requiring the bishop to inquire into the applicant's reasons for departure or dismissal from the prior program. Furthermore, the NCCB's *Program of Priestly Formation, Fourth Edition*, numbers 510 through 528, gives normative regulations concerning applications for formation in this country. Notable among them for these cases are numbers 512, 525, and 526.

Having considered these general prescriptions, as well as the norms presented here for these special cases, if the bishop would like further advice, the Committee on Priestly Formation stands ready to assist him with a review of the application. This review is offered in response to the request by the Congregation for Catholic Education that the episcopal conference set up "a body with the task of studying, upon request of the diocesan bishops, the eventual recourses directed to them, with the scope of providing the bishops with advice to aid their decision." The Committee on Priestly Formation clearly understands this to be a service which it renders, similar to the voluntary visitation program for seminaries. The task of this review process is to render an advisory opinion; recourse can be sought only by the accepting bishop, and the relief offered is review and advice.

This process is an integral part of the internal discipline of the Church by which it assesses the suitability of candidates for priestly formation and seeks to discern answers to what are essentially religious questions. Historically, this process has not been public; rather it has been entirely private and for that reason, confidential. An applicant has a right to a good reputation and the protection of his privacy (c. 220), so any information gained through this procedure and any subsequent review will continue to be held with the highest degree of confidentiality. The process by which the Committee on Priestly Formation might offer fraternal advice to a bishop or major superior will likewise be internal and confidential.

Index

References are to paragraph numbers whenever possible. Entries to indexable material on those few pages without numbered paragraphs, and to the Addendum, are given locators to page numbers, in italics and prefaced by *p.* or *pp.* (*p. 7,* or *pp. 82-85*). Notes are referenced by paragraph number, the letter *n*, and note number (282n168).

Specific citations to canons of the Latin and Eastern Churches may be found under the entry "canonical citations." Specific references to scriptural passages may be found under the entry "biblical citations."

A

academic deans or directors of intellectual formation, 334-336
academic formation. *See* intellectual formation
academic freedom of expression, 365
accreditation and academic standards
    college seminaries, 183
    high school seminaries, 144, 174
    pre-theology programs, 188
    theologate programs, 232
acolytes, 282, 283, 286
Ad gentes divinitus, 239n152, 239n159
Ad pascendum, 282n168
administration of seminaries, 313-343
    business managers, 342
    communication with bishops and religious ordinaries, 295
    directors (*see* directors of formation)
    governance policy, role in, 306
    librarians, 341
    policies, 315
    priests serving as administrators, 306
    public relations and development officers, 342
    qualifications for and responsibilities of those in administrative positions, 306, 307
    rectors (*see* rectors)
    registrars, 336
    role in formation, 314
    secretarial staff, 363
    structure, 313
    vice-rectors, 324
admission of candidates
    academic requirements, 50
    contribution of admissions process to agenda for priestly formation, 40, 46
    dismissal from previous formation program, 62
    diversity, dealing with, 38, 49
    documentation requirements, 39, 47, 63
    financial condition and abilities, 58
    freedom from impediments, determining, 64
    gradualism, principle of, 35-36
    marital status of candidates, determining, 66
    norms for, 42-67
    older applicants, 59
    physical examinations, 65
    previous formation, persons enrolled in (*see* previous formation)
    privacy and confidentiality, 40, 57
    process of, 34-41, 46
    psychological requirements and evaluations, 44, 47, 51-57
    purpose of admissions process, 34

recent conversion or return to
faith, 67
responsibility for oversight of, 39
screening process, 39, 47, 48, 63-67
sexuality, thresholds pertaining
to, 41
statements of policy regarding, 42
thresholds or foundations of
growth and development,
36-37, 43-44
vocation, conviction as to, 45
admissions process, 34-67
adoration of the Blessed Sacrament,
110, 124
advanced study, designation of theologate students for, 235
advisors in formation, 80, 328, 353. See
also directors of formation
affective maturity, 39, 76, 77, 78, 83, 92
AIDS/HIV, 65
alcohol abuse, 64
allergies preventing candidates from
consuming communion elements, 64
amoris officium (work of love), priestly
ministry as, 25
annual reports, 279-282, 326
annual retreats, 122
anthropology, philosophical, 156
asceticism and simplicity of life, 97,
98, 110
St. Augustine, 107

B
background checks, 39, 47
Baptism
documentation required for admission of candidates, 63
priesthood as living-out of baptismal call, 21
Bible
spiritual formation and, 110
theologate program of study, 198-200
biblical and classical languages, 148,
162, 172, 182, 189. See also foreign
language study

biblical citations
2 Corinthians
3:17-18, 68
5:18, 110n76
8:9, 110
Ephesians
5:25, 109n69
5:26-27, 109n69
John
10:10, 109n68
10:17-18, 74n44, 109n68
Luke
5:4, 374
10:42, 20
Mark 10:45, 74n44, 109n67
Matthew
4:18-20, 8
28:19, 9
Philemon 2:6-7a, 110
Psalms 16:5-6, 76n49
1 Timothy 5:22, 308n179
biennium in philosophy, 50, 178, 186
bishops
admissions process, responsibility
for, 39, 286
advanced study, designation of
theologate students for, 235
communication with seminary faculty and administration, 295
continuing formation of priests,
role in, 372, 373
Holy Orders, responsibility for
admission to, 286
magisterial teaching, conformity of
seminaries with, 294
presbyterial communion with, 18
priestly vocations, responsibility
for, 32
rectors, relationship with, 320
release of priests for seminary apostolate, 308, 347
religious seminaries, diocesan priesthood candidates attending, 296
seminary governance, responsibility
for, 291, 293-298, 304, 308

Blessed Sacrament, adoration of,
110, 124
Blessed Virgin Mary, devotion to, 26,
110, 125, 202, 280
boards of seminaries, 299-303
buildings, 309, 310

C

candidacy. *See* admission of
candidates; documentation
canon law
Code of Canon Law (1983), 2, 211
Code of Canons of the Eastern
Churches (1990), 2, 211
theologate study of, 211
canonical citations
CIC (*Codex Iuris Canonici*)
200, *p. 124*
218, 365n198
220, 52n38, 57n40
233, 32n26
233§1, 32n27
239§1, 343n188
239§2, 127n92, 332n186
240§1, 120n83, 120n85
240§2, 120n84, 134n93,
333n187
241, 39, *p. 123*
241§1, 39n33, 44n36
241§2, 39n34, 63
241§3, 61n42, *p. 117*
242§1, *p. vii*
246§1, 116n78
246§2, 117n80
246§3, 125n88
246§4, 120n83, 127n91
246§5, 121n86, 122n87
249, 189n122
250, 50n37, 153n95, 185n119
251, 157n101, 181n116,
188n121
253§1, 344n189, 345n190,
346n193
255, 239n153
256§1, 211n137
258, 239n157

259§2, 293n176
260, 292n175
261, 320n184
262, 312n181, 318n182
264, 312n180
285-286, 64
289, 64
385, 32n30
396-397, 32n32
455, 6n6
455§1, *p. 117*
628, 32n32
748§1, 100n63
750-754, 100n63
818, 345n191
833, 6°, 177n114, 193n124,
283, 319n183
833§7°, 345n192
1028, 283, 285
1031§1, 283, 285
1032§1, 283, 285
1032§2, 285
1033, 63
1034, 283
1034-1035, 282n168
1034§1, 283
1035§1, 283
1035§2, 283
1036, 283, 285
1039, 283, 285
1041, 1°, 64
1041, 2°, 64
1041, 4°, 64
1041, 5°, 64
1041, 6°, 64
1042, 2°, 64
1042, 3°, 64
1050, 63
1050, 1°, 283, 285
1050-52, 282n170
1052§1, 286
CCEO (*Codex Canonum
Ecclesiarum Orientalium*)
10, 100n63
21, 365n198
23, 52n38, 57n40

172§1, 1°, 64
187§2, 283, 345n192
336§1, 293n176
336§2, 312n181, 318n182
338§1, 343n188
338§2, 320n184
339§1, 127n92, 332n186,
    343n188
339§2, 120n83, 120n85
339§3, 120n84, 333n187
339§3, 134n93
340§1, 344n189, 345n190,
    346n193
341, 312n180, 318n182
342§1, 39n33, 44n36
342§2, 39n34, 63
342§3, 61n42
346§2, 120n83
346§2, 2°, 116n78
346§2, 3°, 117n80
346§2, 4° 127n91
346§2, 5°, 125n88
346§2, 6°, 121n86, 122n87
348, 50n37
348§1, 153n95, 185n119
349, 188n121
349§1, 157n101, 181n116
351, 344n189, 345n190,
    346n193
352§2, 239n153
352§§2-3, 211n137
353, 239n157
356§2, 293n176
382-5, 64
598-600, 100n63
644, 345n191
758§1, 5°, 282n169
759, 283
759§1, 285
760, 283
760§1, 285
761, 283, 285
762§1, 1°, 64
762§1, 2°, 64
762§1, 4°, 64
762§1, 5°, 64

762§1, 6°, 64
762§1, 7°, 64
762§1, 8°, 64
769, 1°, 283
769, 3°, 285
769-770, 282n170
769§1, 1°, 63
769§1, 2°, 66
770, 286
772, 283, 285
1436, 100n63
Catechesi tradendae, 203n133
catechesis in theologate curriculum,
    203, 230
Catechism of the Catholic Church
    (1993), 2, 158, 169-170, 187
celibacy and chastity
    affective maturity, 39, 76, 77, 78,
        83, 92
    community rule of life, 269
    discernment of capacity for, 39, 41
    human formation and, 77-79, 90-96
    "the life of priests" and, 26
    spiritual formation and, 110
    sustained period of continence
        prior to admission, 54
    theologate curriculum, 202
child abuse, 41, 55, 64, 96
Christology
    of human formation, 74-76
    ministerial priesthood, foundations
        of, 16, 22-26
    of pastoral formation, 237, 238
    priestly formation grounded in,
        7-9, 374
    of spiritual formation, 107-109
    theologate curriculum, 202
Christus Dominus, 102n65
Church. See also ecclesiology
    historical studies, theologate
        instruction in, 210
    priestly formation in context of,
        10-12, 69
    responsibility for priestly
        vocations, 32

social teaching, theologate instruction in, 208, 229
classical and biblical languages, 148, 162, 172, 182, 189. *See also* foreign language study
codes of canon law. *See* canon law
collaborative seminaries
    directors of intellectual formation, 335
    religious institutes, ventures between, 298
    union-model theologates, collaborative relationships with, 289
college seminaries, 146-159, 175-184
    academic standards and accreditation, 183
    bachelor of arts degree, 175
    liberal arts curriculum, 147-151, 182
    libraries, 184
    norms for, 175-184
    pastoral formation, 256
    philosophy curriculum, 152-157, 176-181
    purpose and goals, 146
    theology curriculum, 158-159, 176, 177, 179-181
Committee on Priestly Formation, 3, *p. 124, pp. ix-x*
Communion. *See* Eucharist
community, 258-271
    balanced life in, 264
    bishop, communion of priests with, 18
    diversity, appreciation of, 271
    ecclesiology of, 258, 259
    governance of seminary, role in, 306
    handbooks, 265, 268
    human formation via, 80
    interpersonal contacts, quality of, 270
    interplay between individual and, 261
    norms for, 263-271
    pastoral formation, as dimension of, 239
    personal and spiritual growth and development rooted in, 260, 262
    rector's conferences, 267
    rule of life, 266
Conference of Major Superiors of Men, statement of, *p. viii*
conferences
    faculty attendance at, 362
    rectorial, 91, 267, 321
Confession. *See* Penance
confessors, 120, 331, *pp. 120*
confidentiality. *See* privacy and confidentiality
Confirmation documentation required for admission of candidates, 63
conflicts regarding theological expression by faculty, resolving, 367
contemplation. *See* personal reflection and meditation
continuing education, theologate programs' stress on need for, 227
continuing evaluation of seminarians, 272-289
    all aspects of priestly formation included in, 275
    annual reports, 279-282, 326
    collaboration with union-model theologates on processes for, 289
    directors of human formation, responsibilities of, 326
    directors of pastoral formation, responsibilities of, 338
    dismissal, 287
    gradualism, principle of, 35-36, 280
    Holy Orders, admission to, 282-286 (*see also* Holy Orders)
    human formation, 280, 326
    intellectual formation, 280
    norms for, 273-289
    pastoral formation, 248, 250, 280, 338
    peer evaluations, 277
    probation and leaves of absence, 288
    procedure for, 274

purpose and goals, 272
responsibility for, 273, 274
self-evaluation, 276
spiritual formation, 280
summer and out-of-term
    activities, 278
continuing evaluation of seminary pro-
    grams by faculty, 361
continuing formation of priests, 368-373
continuing spiritual formation, 110
conversion or return to faith, 67
counseling. See psychological counsel-
    ing, requirements, and evaluations
credo ut intelligam, 136
criminal background checks, 39, 47, 64
cultural preparation programs, 140, 160
cultural sensitivities. See diversity

D
days of recollection, 110, 121, 122, 331
deans. See directors of formation
degrees offered
    college seminaries, 175
    pre-theology programs, 190
    theologate programs, 231, 232
Dei verbum, 198n127, 200n129
development and growth of candidates.
    See thresholds or foundations of
    growth and development
development and public relations.
    See "public relations and develop-
    ment," under seminaries
development of faculty, 349
devotional prayer, spiritual formation
    via, 110, 124, 125
diaconate. See Holy Orders
diocesan bishops. See bishops
diocesan priesthood, 19. See also priest-
    hood, nature and mission of
directors of formation
    academic dean or director of intel-
        lectual formation, 334-336
    formation mentors/advisors, 80,
        328, 353
    human formation, 80, 325-327
    pastoral formation, 245, 256, 337-340

spiritual formation
    directors of, 329-331
    individual spiritual directors
        (see spiritual directors)
directors of vocations, 32, 39, 48
Directory for the Application of Principles
    and Norms on Ecumenism, 224
dismissals
    of candidates for admission from
        previous formation programs,
        62, pp. 119-120
    from seminary program, 287
diversity, 12. See also foreign
    language study
    admission of candidates, 38, 49
    community life and, 271
    cultural preparation programs, 160
    English language, adequate com-
        mand of, 49, 160, 172, 182
    faculty, 354, 355
    in high school seminaries, 145, 167
    intellectual formation, 140, 145,
        160, 167
    pastoral formation and, 239, 252
    in theologate programs, 228
doctrinal responsibilities. See magisterial
    teaching, conformity with
documentation
    admission to priestly candidacy,
        requirements for, 39, 47, 63
    priestly formation or religious life,
        persons previously enrolled in,
        pp. 120-122
    registrars responsible for, 336
documents pertinent to priestly
    formation, 1-3
dogmatic theology, 202
drug abuse, 64, 65
dysfunctional families, candidates
    from, 12, 53

E
Eastern Churches
    Code of Canons of the Eastern
        Churches (1990), 2, 211 (see also
        under canonical citations)

marital status of priestly candidates in, 66

minor orders and diaconate, requirements for conferral of, 283

PPF as normative for, 6n6

in theologate study, 211, 223

Ecclesia de Eucharistia, 26, 32n31, 76n47, 118, 213n139

Ecclesia in America, 1, 12, 110

ecclesiology
    of community, 258, 259
    foundations of ministerial priesthood in, 16
    pastoral formation, essential elements of, 239
    of priestly formation, 10-12, 69
    of spiritual formation, 109, 110
    theologate curriculum, 202, 222

ecumenism
    pastoral formation and, 239, 247
    spiritual formation, ecumenical events as part of, 126
    in theologate programs, 163, 216, 224

endowments, 312

English language, adequate command of, 49, 160, 172, 182

enrollment levels, monitoring, 311

epistemology, study of, 156

Erga migrantes, 239n159

eschatology, 202

Essential Norms (2002), 12

ethical standards in U.S. society, 12

ethics and moral theology, 156, 204-209

Eucharist
    admission to candidacy and regular partaking of, 37
    adoration of the Blessed Sacrament, 110, 124
    allergies preventing candidates from consuming communion elements, 64
    pastoral formation and, 239
    priesthood, nature and mission of, 16, 24, 26
    priestly vocations and, 32

seminaries and, 290, 321, 331, 352

spiritual formation and, 110, 116, 118, 119, 280

theologate programs and, 214, 215

evaluations
    for admission (*see* admission of candidates)
    continuing (*see* continuing evaluation of seminarians)
    continuing evaluation of seminary programs by faculty, 361
    of faculty, 359
    persons previously enrolled in priestly formation or religious life, *pp. 119-124*
    psychological (*see* psychological counseling, requirements, and evaluations)

evangelization
    pastoral formation, essential elements of, 239
    theologate curriculum, 203

F

facilities, 309, 310

faculty, 344-367
    appointment and approval, 345
    communication with bishops and religious ordinaries, 295
    conditions of service, 344-357
    conflicts regarding theological expression, resolving, 367
    continuing evaluation of seminary programs by, 361
    dedication to formation of students, 351, 353
    diversity, 354, 355
    evaluation of, 359
    freedom of expression by, 365
    governance of seminary, role in, 306
    handbooks, 358, 367
    lay persons, role of, 348, 350
    liturgy and sacraments, participation in, 352

magisterial teaching, conformity
with, 345, 364-367
meetings and committees, 360
as models for seminarians, 104,
351-357
organization of, 358-363
pastoral involvement of, 357
planning and development, 349
priestly status, 347
Profession of Faith by, 193, 345
professional qualifications, 346
sabbaticals, conference attendance,
and study leaves, 362
secretaries, 363
social teaching of Church, awareness of, 356
as spiritual directors and formation
mentors/advisors, 353
faith. *See also* Oath of Fidelity;
Profession of Faith
foundations of priestly formation in
truths of, 13-14
recent conversion or return to, 67
in theologate programs, 222, 225-226
families
dysfunctional families, candidates
from, 12, 53
responsibility for priestly
vocations, 32
theologate study of, 218
Fides et ratio
college seminaries, study of philosophy in, 152n94, 153n96,
156n98, 157n102-103, 178n115
pre-theologate, study of philosophy
in, 186n120
fides quaerens intellectum, 163
fiduciary and financial responsibilities
of seminaries, 303, 308, 312, 343
field experience. *See* practical experience and onsite programs *under*
pastoral formation
financial condition and abilities of
candidates, 58
first pastoral assignments, 372

foreign language study
classical and biblical languages,
148, 162, 172, 182, 189
college seminary programs, 148, 182
continuing evaluation of seminarians, 280
high school seminary programs, 172
pastoral formation and, 252
pre-theology programs, 162, 189
Spanish language, 162, 172,
182, 228
theologate programs, 228
formation, priestly. *See*
priestly formation
formators. *See* directors of formation
foundations of growth and development. *See* thresholds or foundations
of growth and development
freedom of expression, academic, 365
freedom of priestly candidates from
impediments, determining, 64
fundamental theology, 197

G
Gaudium et Spes, 136
gluten allergies, 64
Gospel, priestly life as witness to radicalism of, 26
governance of seminaries. *See*
under seminaries
gradualism, principle of, 35-36, 280
graduate theology. *See*
theologate programs
Great Jubilee, 11, 12
Greek and Latin, 148, 162, 172, 182,
189. *See also* foreign
language study
growth and development of
faculty, 349
growth and development of seminarians. *See* thresholds or foundations
of growth and development
growth and public relations. *See* public
relations and development
under seminaries

H

handbooks
of community life, 5n5, 265, 268, 273
for faculty, 358, 367
Hebrew and other biblical languages, 148, 162, 172, 182, 189. *See also* foreign language study
high school seminaries, 142-145, 165-174
academic standards and accreditation, 144, 174
college preparatory program, 171, 173
diversity in, 145, 167
norms for, 165-174
pastoral formation, 257
purpose and goals, 142-144
religious instruction in, 169-170
historical-critical method, 200
historical studies, theologate instruction in, 210
history of philosophy, 155
HIV/AIDS, 65
Holy Orders. *See also* priesthood, nature and mission of
annual evaluations and advancement in, 282
requirements for conferral
of diaconate, 283
of priesthood, 285
suitability to receive diaconate based on judgments regarding suitability for priesthood, 284
theologate curriculum on, 202
Holy See, directives of, 292
homiletics
pastoral formation, proclamation of the Word as essential element of, 239
in theologate programs, 200, 215
homosexual experiences or tendencies, 56
human formation, 74-105
age and stage of person in formation, 81
candidate's responsibility for, 87
celibacy and chastity, preparation for, 77-79, 90-96
characteristics instilled by, 76
Christology of, 74-76
continuing evaluations, 280, 326
directors of, 80, 325-327
formation mentors and advisors, 80
integration with other dimensions of formation, 73, 82
interiorization, evidence of, 86
methods for fostering, 80
models, seminary faculty as, 104
norms for, 83-105
obedience, preparation for, 100-102
philosophy, study of, 154
priesthood, focus on, 84
psychological counseling, requirements, and evaluations, 76, 80, 89, 105
purpose and goals of, 85-86
seminaries, via life of, 80
seminary program of, 83-84, 103-105
sexuality, 77-79, 90-96
simplicity of life, preparation for, 97, 98
spiritual directors and, 80, 131
thresholds or foundations of, 88-89

I

immigrants in U.S. society, 12. *See also* diversity
impediments, determining freedom of priestly candidates from, 64
integration of dimensions of formation
human formation, 73, 82
intellectual formation, 73, 136, 164
pastoral formation, 73, 241
spiritual formation, 73, 106, 112-114
intellectual formation, 136-235
admission to candidacy, academic requirements for, 50
context of, 140

continuing evaluation in annual reports, 280

cultural preparation programs, 140, 160

defined, 136-137

directors of (academic deans), 334-336

graduate theology (see theologate programs)

in high school (see high school seminaries)

integration with other dimensions of formation, 73, 136, 164

magisterial teaching, conformity with, 180, 193, 222

norms for, 165-235

pre-theologate (see pre-theology programs)

priestly ministry, orientation towards, 138

stages of, 141

undergraduate programs (see college seminaries)

intention of priestly candidates, 37

J

John Paul II. See also specific communications, e.g., Pastores dabo vobis

on seminary formation, 7

seminary visitations mandated by, 4

L

Laetamur magnopere, 158n104

languages. See also foreign language study

classical and biblical languages, 148, 162, 172, 182, 189

English language, adequate command of, 49, 160, 172, 182

Spanish language, study of, 162, 172, 182, 228

Latin and Greek, 148, 162, 172, 182, 189. See also foreign language study

lay persons, role of, 308, 348, 350

leadership development and pastoral formation, 239

leaves of absence

faculty study leaves, 288

probation, seminarians on, 288

lectio divina, 110, 123

lectorate, 282, 283, 286

liberal arts curriculum, college seminaries, 147-151, 182

librarians, 341

libraries, 184, 233, 310

"the life of priests," concept of, 20-31. See also priesthood, nature and mission of

liturgical life of seminary, 116-126, 331, 352

liturgical studies in theologate programs, 213-214

Liturgy of the Hours

continuing evaluation of seminarians and, 280, 283

directors of spiritual formation and, 331

spiritual formation, 110, 117, 119, 280

logic, study of, 156

Lumen gentium, 2n1, 21n14, 26n19, 242n160

M

magisterial teaching, conformity with. See also Oath of Fidelity; Profession of Faith

college seminaries, instruction at, 180

faculty responsibilities, 345

Profession of Faith by teachers in theologate programs, 193

seminaries, responsibilities of bishops and religious ordinaries regarding, 294

theologate program, 222

Marialis cultus, 125n89

marital status of candidates, determining, 66

marriage and family, theologate study of, 218

Mary, devotion to, 26, 110, 125, 202, 280

mature applicants, 12, 59

medical-moral ethics, 206
meditation. *See* personal reflection
   and meditation
mentors
   first pastoral assignments, 372
   in formation, 80, 328, 353 (*see also*
      directors of formation)
metaphysics, study of, 156
Ministeria quaedam, 282n168
ministerial priesthood. *See* priesthood,
   nature and mission of; priestly formation; priestly vocations
ministries of acolyte and lector, 282,
   283, 286
minor orders. *See* Holy Orders
missiology, theologate study of, 202
mission statements of seminaries,
   265, 305
missionary dimension of pastoral formation, 239
moral relativism in U.S. society, 12
moral theology and ethics, 156, 204-209
multiculturalism. *See* diversity
Mutuae relationes, 31n25

N
natural theology, study of, 156, 178, 186
nature, study of philosophy of, 156
Novo millennio ineunte, 1, 11n9

O
Oath of Fidelity
   diaconate, ordination to, 283
   faculty, 345
   priesthood, ordination to, 285
   rectors, 319
obedience
   human formation and, 100-102
   spiritual formation and, 110
older applicants, 12, 59
onsite experience. *See* practical experience and onsite programs *under*
   pastoral formation
ongoing processes. *See entries*
   at continuing

Optatam totius
   as document important to
      priestly formation, 2
   faculty of seminaries, 344n189
   human formation, 79n52, 80n57
   intellectual formation
      in college seminaries, 157n102,
         182n117-118
      in pre-theologate, 189n122,
         189n123
      in theologate, 203n134,
         205n135, 219n143
   pastoral formation, 238
   rectors, 322n185
   on seminary faculties, 345n190
   spiritual formation, 107
Orders and ordination. *See*
   Holy Orders
Orthodox Churches. *See*
   Eastern Churches

P
papacy, directives of, 292
pastoral formation, 236-257
   Christology of, 237, 238
   college seminaries, 256
   continuing evaluations, 248, 250,
      280, 338
   as culmination of formation pro-
      cess, 236
   directors of, 245, 256, 337-340
   diversity, awareness of, 239, 252
   essential elements and characteris-
      tics of, 239
   faculty involvement, 357
   formal seminary program for, 242-
      246
   high school seminaries, 257
   integration with other dimensions
      of formation, 73, 241
   local diocese and presbyterate,
      familiarity with, 239, 247, 254
   norms for, 242-257
   personal reflection and meditation,
      248, 253
   philosophy, study of, 154

poor, working with, 239, 251
practical experience and onsite
    programs, 239
    broad exposure, need for, 246
    college seminaries, 256
    directors of pastoral formation,
        responsibilities of, 339, 340
    diversity, exposure to, 252
    faculty involvement, 357
    high school seminaries, 257
    poor, working with, 251
    pre-theology programs, 255
    responsibility for providing, 247
    supervisors of, 249, 339
pre-theology programs, 255
purpose and goal of, 238, 244
supervisors of, 240, 248, 249, 253,
    255, 339
in theologate programs, 196
theological reflection, 248
pastoral theology, theologate study of,
    217, 218
Pastores dabo vobis
    academic qualifications for admis-
        sion of candidates, 50n37
    admissions process, 34, 37
    celibacy and chastity, 78, 79n53,
        90n61
    Christological foundations
        of human formation, 74-76
        of ministerial priesthood, 16,
            22, 23, 26
    community, 259n162
    context of priestly formation and,
        7n7, 11
    continuing formation of priests,
        369, 370
    as document crucial to priestly
        formation, 1
    ecclesiological foundations of min-
        isterial priesthood, 17
    governance of seminaries, 291,
        308n179
    human formation
        celibacy and chastity, 78,
            79n53, 90n61
        directors of, 325

intellectual formation, 136, 137
    for college seminaries, 154,
        157n102, 178n115
    for pre-theologate, 186n120
    for theologate, 163n107-113,
        196n125, 217n141
    "the life of priests," 22, 23, 26
pastoral formation, 236, 238,
    239n154-156, 239n158
presbyteral communion with bish-
    ops, 18
program of formation in seminaries,
    need for, 70
psychological evaluation of candi-
    dates, 57n41
responsibility for priestly
    vocations, 32
seminaries, 290n174
seminary faculty, 348n195,
    351n196, 364n197, 367n200
spiritual formation, 106, 107,
    110n71-75
Trinitarian foundations of ministe-
    rial priesthood, 15
patristics and patrology, 201
peace, fostering spirit of, 110
pedagogical methods used in theolo-
    gate programs, 234
peer evaluations, 277
peer relationships in first pastoral
    assignments, 372
Penance
    admission to candidacy and regular
        partaking of, 37
    celibacy and chastity, fostering, 79
    confessors, 120, 331
    continuing evaluation of seminar-
        ians, 283
    directors of spiritual formation, 331
    intellectual formation, 205, 214
    spiritual formation and, 110, 120,
        134, 280
Perfectae caritatis, 29n24
personal reflection and meditation
    human formation via, 80
    pastoral formation, 248, 253
    spiritual formation, 110, 121, 122

Philippinas insulas, 125n89
philosophy
    academic requirements for admission to candidacy regarding, 50
    college seminary curriculum, 152-157, 176-181
    content of curriculum, 155-157
    diaconate candidates, 283
    four dimensions of formation, relationship to, 154
    liberal arts and, 151
    pre-theology programs, 50, 161, 185-186
    priesthood, ordination to, 285
    priestly formation and, 155
    theologate formation in, 192
    theology and, 152-153
physical examination of candidates, 65
physical plant, 309, 310
planning
    continuing formation of priests, 370
    seminary faculty, 349
    seminary governance, 307-312
the poor
    pastoral formation and working with, 239, 251
    preferential option for, 239
poverty and simplicity of life, 97, 98, 110
PPF. *See Program of Priestly Formation*
practical experience. *See under* pastoral formation
prayer, 110, 116-126. *See also* personal reflection and meditation
pre-theology programs, 161-162, 185-190
    academic standards, 188
    admissions process, 46
    bachelor in philosophy (PhB) degree, 190
    gradualism, principle of, 35
    norms for, 185-190
    pastoral formation, 255
    philosophy curriculum, 50, 161, 185-186
    previous formation, candidates without, 60

purpose and goals, 161-162
    theology curriculum, 161, 187
preferential option for the poor, 239
presbyterate. *See* priesthood, nature and mission of
Presbyterorum ordinis
    as document important to priestly formation, 2n1
    human formation, 76n50, 99n62, 102n64
    "the life of priests" and, 20, 25, 26n17, 26n19
    pastoral formation, 239n149
previous formation
    candidates successfully completing earlier stages of formation, 61
    candidates without any previous formation experiences, 60
    priestly formation or religious life, persons previously enrolled in, *pp. 117-124*
    acceptance of, *p. 122*
    departure letters, *p. 119*
    dismissal from, 62, *pp. 119-120*
    evaluation of applicants, *pp. 119-124*
    purpose of norms for, *pp. 118-119*
    rejection of, *p. 120, p. 123*
    release of relevant information, *pp. 119-121*
    reservations regarding, *p. 123*
    specific inquiries on application forms regarding, *p. 120*
    waiting period, 62, *pp. 119-120*
priesthood, nature and mission of, 13-14. *See also* Holy Orders
    baptismal call, as part of, 21
    Christological foundations, 16, 22-26
    communion of priests with bishop, 18
    communion with bishop, 18
    continuing formation of priests, 368-373

diocesan *vs.* religious context, 19,
26-30
ecclesiological foundations, 17
human formation program's focus
on, 84
intellectual formation oriented
towards, 138
"the life of priests," concept of,
20-31
requirements for admission to
priesthood, 285
responsibility for priestly
vocations, 32
spiritual formation as preparation
for, 109
suitability to receive diaconate
based on judgments regarding
suitability for priesthood, 284
theologate curriculum on Holy
Orders, 202
transition programs into priesthood, 370
Trinitarian foundations, 15
priestly formation
admission to (*see* admission
of candidates)
Christology of, 7-9, 374
continuing formation of priests,
368-373
defined, 68
ecclesiological context, 10-12, 69
faculty dedication to, 351, 353
four dimensions or pillars of, 68-73
(*see also* human formation; intellectual formation; pastoral formation; spiritual formation)
goals of, 71
nature and mission of ministerial
priesthood, foundation in,
13-19
philosophy, study of, 155
previous enrollment (*see* previous
formation)
seminary program fostering, 70 (*see
also* seminaries)

theologate programs focused
on, 195
truths of faith as foundation of,
13-14
worldly context, 10-12
priestly vocations
admission, norms for, 45
discernment of, 33
recent conversion or return to
faith, 67
responsibility for, 32
as specific vocation, 22
vocation directors, 32, 39, 48
privacy and confidentiality
admissions process, 40, 57
persons previously enrolled in
priestly formation or religious
life, *p. 121, p. 124*
spiritual directors, 134, 135, 333
probation, 288
proclamation of the Word
homiletics as part of theologate
program, 200, 215
pastoral formation, as essential element of, 239
Profession of Faith
diaconate candidates, 283
faculty, 193, 345
rectors, 319
professional ethics, 156, 204-209
professors. *See* faculty
Program of Priestly Formation (PPF)
administrators of seminaries, role
of, 307
documents pertinent to, 1-3
editions of, 1, 4, *pp. ix-x*
promulgation of, *p. vii*
responsibility of bishop or religious
ordinary for implementation
of, 293
responsibility of individual religious
institutes and societies for
implementation of, 297
seminary visitations contributing
to, 4-6

psychological counseling, requirements, and evaluations
    admission to candidacy, 44, 47, 51-57
    directors of human formation, responsibilities of, 325, 327
    human formation, 76, 80, 89, 105
    spiritual formation, 110
public relations and development. *See under* seminaries

R

Ratio fundamentalis institutionis sacerdotalis (1970, 1985), 2, 39, 264n164, 347n194, *p. vii*
recent conversion or return to faith, 67
recollection, days of, 110, 122
reconciliation, fostering spirit of, 110
records. *See* documentation
rectors, 318-323
    administrative responsibilities, 323
    admission of candidates, responsibilities regarding, 39, 57, 65
    annual reports on seminarians, 279
    appointment of, 319
    community life, 267
    conferences, 91, 267, 321
    diaconate candidates, verifications regarding, 283
    faculty, appointment and approval of, 345
    governance policy, responsibility for, 304
    human formation, 80, 84, 91, 103, 105
    Magisterium, conformity of college seminary teaching with teaching of, 180
    priestly ordinands, verifications regarding, 285
    priestly vocations, discernment of, 32
    priests serving as, 318
    psychological counseling, requirements, and evaluation, 57, 105
    spiritual responsibilities of, 127, 135, 320-322
    vice-rectors, 324
Redemptoris missio, 26n23, 239n151
reference checks, 39, 47
reflection. *See* personal reflection and meditation
registrars, 336
release of priests for seminary apostolate, 308, 347
religious orders
    advanced study, designation of theologate students for, 235
    charism of founder, identification with, 29-31
    collaborative ventures between different institutes, 298
    diocesan priesthood candidates attending seminaries of, 296
    "the life of priests" in, 26-31
    nature and mission of, 19
    previous formation in (*see* previous formation)
    priesthood, nature and mission of, 19, 26-30
    regulation of formation process by individual institutes and societies, 297
    statement of Conference of Major Superiors of Men, *p. viii*
religious ordinaries
    admissions process, responsibility for, 39
    communication with seminary faculty and administration, 295
    Holy Orders, responsibility for admission to, 286
    magisterial teaching, conformity of seminaries with, 294
    rectors, relationship with, 320
    release of priests for seminary apostolate, 308, 347
    seminary governance, responsibility for, 291, 293-298, 304, 308
reports, annual, 279-282, 326

retreats
    diaconate, prior to admission
      to, 283
    priesthood, prior to admission
      to, 285
    spiritual formation and annual
      retreats, 110, 122
return to faith, 67
review processes. *See* evaluations
right intention of priestly candidates, 37
Rosarium Virginis Mariae, 125n89-90
rosary, 110, 124, 125
rule of life, 266, 269, 294

S
sabbaticals for faculty, 362
sacraments. *See also* specific sacra-
    ments, e.g., Penance
    college seminary curriculum,
      158, 179
    faculty participation in, 351
    liturgical life of seminary, 116-126
    pastoral formation, sacramental
      dimension of, 239
    pre-theologate curriculum, 187
    theologate curriculum, 202, 211
Sacrosanctum concilium, 26n21
Sapientia christiana, 345n191
screening of applicants for admission,
    39, 47, 48, 63-67
Scripture. *See also* biblical citations
    spiritual formation and, 110
    theologate program of study,
      198-200
Second Vatican Council, 2, 11, 20,
    29, 163, 182, 189. *See also* specific
    documents, e.g., *Lumen gentium*
secretarial staff, 363
self-evaluation, 276
self-knowledge and insight, 54, 76, 79,
    80, 280
seminarians
    communication of contents of
      annual report to, 281
    continuing evaluation of (*see*
      continuing evaluation
      of seminarians)

    dismissal of, 287
    governance of seminary, role in, 306
    responsibility for priestly
      vocations, 32
seminaries, 290-367. *See also* collabora-
    tive seminaries; college seminaries;
    high school seminaries; pre-theol-
    ogy programs; theologate programs
    administration (*see* administration
      of seminaries)
    admission to (*see* admission
      of candidates)
    bishops, responsibilities of, 291,
      293-298, 304, 308
    boards, 299-303
    business managers, 342
    communication of bishops and reli-
      gious with faculty and adminis-
      tration, 295
    continuing evaluation of seminar-
      ians, responsibility for, 273, 274
    continuing formation of priests,
      role in, 370, 371
    cultural preparation programs,
      140, 160
    diocesan priesthood candidates
      attending religious
      seminaries, 296
    directors (*see* directors of formation)
    dismissal from, 287
    endowments, 312
    enrollment levels, monitoring, 311
    facilities, 309, 310
    faculty (*see* faculty)
    fiduciary and financial responsibili-
      ties, 303, 308, 312, 343
    governance of, 291-292
      bishops and religious ordinaries,
        291, 293-298, 304, 308
      boards, 299-303
      planning, 307-312
      policy as to, 302, 304-306
      seminary community's role
        in, 306
    handbooks, 265, 268
    human formation, program of,
      83-84, 103-105

human formation via life of, 80
librarians, 341
libraries, 184, 233, 310
liturgical life of, 116-126
magisterial teaching, conformity
  with, 294
mission statements, 305
pastoral formation, supervision
  of, 240
planning
  continuing formation of
    priests, 370
  faculty, 349
  governance, 307-312
program of priestly formation, need
  for, 70
public relations and development
  administrative officer in charge
    of, 342
  governance planning require-
    ments, 307-312
  rector, role of, 320
rectors (see rectors)
registrars, 336
religious institutes and societies,
  regulation of formation process
  by, 297
religious ordinaries, responsibilities
  of, 291, 293-298, 304, 308
responsibility for priestly
  vocations, 32
rule of life, 266, 269
spiritual formation as heart of, 115
vice-rectors, 324
visitations of, 4-6
sexual ethics in theologate
  curriculum, 207
sexuality. See also celibacy and chastity
  admission of candidates and mat-
    ters of, 41, 55, 56
  affective maturity, 39, 76, 77, 78,
    83, 92
  child abuse and, 41, 55, 64, 96
  homosexual experiences or
    tendencies, 56
  human formation and, 77-79
  self-knowledge regarding, 93

simplicity of life, 97-99, 110, 269, 280
social teaching of Church, 208,
  229, 356
society. See world and society
solidarity, fostering spirit of, 110
solitude, 79, 93, 110, 121, 266
Spanish language, study of, 162, 172,
  182, 228. See also foreign
  language study
spiritual directors, 127-135, 332-333
  approval and appointment, 127
  candidates dismissed from previous
    formation program, p. 120
  directors of spiritual formation,
    329-331
  faculty serving as, 351, 353
  first pastoral assignments, 372
  human formation via, 80, 131
  as means of spiritual formation, 110
  meetings with, 127, 133, 135
  Penance, 120
  privacy and confidentiality, 134, 135
  regular meetings with, 127
spiritual formation, 106-135
  apostolic dimensions of, 110
  Bible study, 110
  celibacy and chastity, 110
  Christological aspects of, 107-109
  continuing evaluation in annual
    reports, 280
  continuing nature of, 110
  defined, 107-109
  devotional prayer and, 110,
    124, 125
  director of, 329-331
  directors in (see spiritual directors)
  ecclesiology of, 109
  Eucharist and, 110, 116, 118,
    119, 280
  as heart of seminary life, 115
  integration with other dimensions
    of formation, 73, 106, 112-114
  Liturgy of the Hours, 110, 117,
    119, 280
  methods of, 110, 111
  norms for, 116-135
  obedience and, 110

ongoing, 110
Penance and, 110, 120, 134, 280
personal reflection and meditation, 110, 121, 122
philosophy, study of, 154
practices and devotions fostering, 110
prayer as means of, 110, 116-126
priestly nature of, 109
psychological characteristics fostered by, 110
reconciling spirit, fostering, 110
rectors, responsibilities of, 127, 135, 320-322
retreats and days of recollection, 110, 122
simplicity of life and asceticism, 110
solidarity, fostering, 110
solitude, 110, 121
Trinitarian foundations of, 107, 108
spirituality and spiritual direction, theologate study of, 212
study leaves for faculty, 288
substance abuse, 64
synchronic methods of study of Scripture, 200

T
teachers. *See* faculty
teaching principles, methods, and skills, theologate instruction in, 230
theologate programs, 163, 191-235
academic standards, 232
advanced study, designation of students for, 235
annual retreats, 122
Bible, study of, 198-200
canon law, 211
catechesis, 203, 230
catechesis and evangelization, 203
continuing education, stress on need for, 227
continuing formation of priests, as foundation for, 370
degrees offered, 231, 232

diverse society, recognition of needs of, 228
dogmatic theology, 202
Eastern Churches, study of, 211, 223
ecclesiology, 202, 222
ecumenism, 163, 216, 224
faith, recognition of basis of theology in, 222, 225-226
fundamental theology, 197
historical studies, 210
homiletics, 200, 215
length of study, 191
library, 233
liturgical studies, 213-214
Magisterium, normative function of, 222
methodologies, instruction in, 219-221
moral theology, 204-209
norms for, 191-235
pastoral formation and, 196
pastoral theology, 217, 218
patristics and patrology, 201
pedagogical methods, 234
philosophical formation required for, 192
previous formation, candidates without, 60
priestly formation as focus of, 195
profession of faith by teachers in, 193
purpose and goals, 163
social teaching of Church, instruction in, 208, 229
spirituality and spiritual direction, 212
teaching principles, methods, and skills, instruction in, 230
Thomism, stress on, 219
undergraduate theology coursework as preparation for, 159
union-model theologates, collaborative relationships with, 289
unity of academic curriculum, 194

theology
    diaconate candidates, 283
    doctrinal responsibilities and teach-
        ing of (see magisterial teaching,
        conformity with)
    graduate (see theologate programs)
    high school seminaries, religious
        instruction in, 169-170
    liberal arts and study of, 149
    natural theology, study of, 156
    philosophy and, 152-153
    pre-theologate, 161, 187
    priesthood, ordination to, 285
    undergraduate curriculum,
        158-159, 176, 177, 179-181
St. Thomas Aquinas, 157, 157n102, 219
thresholds or foundations of growth
    and development
    admission of candidates, 36-37,
        43-44
    community as basis of, 260, 262
    human formation, 88-89
transition programs into
    priesthood, 370
Trinitarian foundations
    of ministerial priesthood, 15
    of spiritual formation, 107, 108

U

union-model theologates, collaborative
    relationships with, 289
Unitatis redintegratio, 163n112
United States Conference of Catholic
    Bishops (USCCB), directives
    of, 292

V

Vatican Council II, 2, 11, 20, 29, 163,
    182, 189. See also specific docu-
    ments, e.g., Lumen gentium
Veritatis splendor, 76n46, 205n135
vice-rectors, 324
Virgin Mary, devotion to, 26, 110, 125,
    202, 280
visitations to seminaries, 4-6
vocation directors, 32, 39, 48
vocations. See priestly vocations

W

waiting period for candidates dismissed
    from previous formation program,
    62, pp. 119-120
wheat allergies, 64
workshops, 122, 355
the world and society
    intellectual formation in context
        of, 140
    liberal arts curriculum in college
        seminaries and, 150
    pre-theology programs in context
        of, 162
    priestly formation in context
        of, 12
    social teaching of Church, theolo-
        gate instruction in, 208, 229
    solidarity, fostering spirit of, 110